FIRE IN YOUR PULPIT

*F*IRE
IN YOUR
*P*ULPIT

Dr. Robert G. Delnay

Piedmont Baptist College Press
716 Franklin Street
Winston-Salem, North Carolina 27101
Phone (336) 725-8344

www.pbc.edu

Fire in Your Pulpit was originally published and copyrighted by Regular Baptist Press, Schaumburg, Illinois.

Library of Congress Cataloging-in-Publication Data

Delnay, Robert G.,
      Fire in Your Pulpit / Robert G. Delnay
           p. cm.
        ISBN 0-9708261-0-9
BV4211.2.D379   1990   90-38649
251-dc20   CIP

©1990 Regular Baptist Press
Schaumburg, Illinois

©2001 Piedmont Baptist College Press
Winston-Salem, North Carolina

To my parents,
Sophie and George Delnay.

CONTENTS

Introduction 9

1. What Right Do You Have to Say That? 15

2. Finding the Burden...23

3. Preaching Is for Decision 29

4. Confidence from Your Exegesis 35

5. Confidence in Your Organization 43

6. Clear Motives...53

7. Illustrations That Burn.......................................59

8. On Getting Interest 67

9. What Does Delivery Have to Do with It? 79

10. On Being a Communicator 89

11. Any Concern? Any Passion? Any Tears?.............97

12. Imagination in Preaching 107

13. How Does Suggestion Work? 117

14. Clear Phrasing 127

15. The Textual Sermon 135

16. Authority in Your Preaching 141

17. Wrapping It Up—And on Time.........................149

A Last Word 157

INTRODUCTION

It is an experience I hope you've had—and had lately: You were preaching with liberty. You knew that your message was faithful to Scripture. You had the confidence that comes from above because you had the authority of both a divine call and a divine enabling. Your words were coming in a torrent. Not only that, your people were with you. You knew you were communicating.

You probably had the confidence that you had laid your foundation. You had done your exegesis on your passage, and you had studied the pivotal words. You had looked up the background material on the passage, and you knew the setting in which it was written. You had read your commentaries and had thought about the problems in the passage. In the process you had gained fresh insights, and as you had reflected on the passage, you gained more insights. You had the confidence that you had studied.

In addition to this confidence, you knew that you had your message together. You had mulled it over long enough that you knew it was clear in your own mind. You had organized the material into a unified, coherent statement. You had the insights and the illustrations to make it clear and compelling.

Not only that, you knew that your heart was right. So far as you know your own motives, you look back with the confidence that you weren't trying to impress men. You were there to serve God. At the same time, you knew that you had a genuine concern for your people. Whether by a smile or by tears, that concern impelled you. You knew that you had the message they needed.

And now as you look back, it's a profound satisfaction, isn't it?

If our experience tells us that it's not quite that way every time— even with the purest men we know—our hearts will agree that it is still an ideal that every preacher should work toward. We do yearn to score every time we preach. We do yearn that through our preaching God would save lost people and change lives. And I repeat, such a ministry gives profound satisfaction.

Why Passion?

"And they were not able to resist the wisdom and the spirit by which he spake" (Acts 6:10).

Introduction

Listen to almost any large sampling of preaching in the second half of this century, and you risk the impression that Stephen's kind of preaching must be rare. Who gets to hear preaching that cuts to the heart the way his did or the way Peter's did? Instead of getting pulpit fire, many congregations seem to be getting bland fare, delivered with all the intensity of a weather report. Isaiah preached after his lips had touched the hot coal from off the altar. Many a sermon now comes from lips that have touched nothing hotter than a cup of lukewarm chocolate.

All too often it is Sunday morning in Dullsville. The preacher, however much we may like him, speaks his message with a curious lack of intensity. Curious, because preaching is supposed to convey the Word of God to eternal souls, and we would expect some urgency in carrying out such a dread task. We might expect passion at the greatness of God or anger at human sin. We might expect tears or at least anxious concern at the spiritual danger our people live in or at the griefs that many of them suffer.

There is such a thing as psyching oneself up to fervency the way that a weight lifter meditates in silence before he goes down for the bar. If a preacher attempts this in the energy of the flesh, he would do well to reread Leviticus 10; here Nadab and Abihu offered fire that they had not taken from off the altar. God did not like it; He struck them dead for it. He forbade pouring anointing oil on man's flesh, and we can't very well expect Him to anoint our flesh with Holy Spirit power. Scratch the idea of psyching yourself up. God did not call His prophets to be actors.

There is also such a thing as cultural conditioning. In some parts of the country a preacher moves into a kind of passionate discourse as easily as an auctioneer begins his chant. It is a preaching pattern that he has accepted from all his models, and his intensity expresses not so much his feeling for his message as the religious culture he represents. If it had to be a choice between the Nadab and the auctioneer, surely the Lord would find the auctioneer easier to forgive. But if any man lack fire, just moving to another part of the country and to a different culture is not likely of itself to warm him much. Honest intensity comes by a different path.

O Preacher, we take our places in front of your pulpit to hear a message fresh from God. We come preoccupied and often careless. Some of us are sleepy from late work or late entertainment. Few of us have met God this morning or this week in any prolonged encounter. We are taken up with things, with our hopes and with our problems, some of them trivial and some of them devastating. We sit here waiting for your message. We do not need a performance or a display of your learning. We need a word from God, a word that has so moved you that it will move us. We expect that you have prepared faithfully and specifically to give us this word; and we ask that you have prepared your own heart so that God can use you as His messenger. We ask that you have met God, confessing your sins and cleansing your motives, and that you mount your platform in the holy confidence that you are coming to us directly from being with Him. Whatever your sermon, cheerful or somber, we ask that it be true to the Word of God and that you deliver it to us with holy fire burning in your bones.

Should we insist that real preaching in some way carries intensity? As people commonly use the term "preaching," it has several connotations.

1. Preaching is for decision. Just as teaching is primarily to instruct, preaching is primarily to persuade. Teaching tries to convey truths, skills and values. Preaching tries to generate resolves. A teacher may indeed persuade, but to him persuasion is secondary. A preacher may instruct; indeed we expect him to. But to him persuasion is more important.
2. Preaching is normally uninterrupted discourse. Teaching often involves give and take, and most lecturers permit questions from the class. By custom, preachers expect that they will carry straight on through their sermons, and most of us cannot remember how long it has been since we were interrupted or heckled.
3. Preaching requires intensity. A teacher may instruct in a quiet voice and laid-back manner and still be highly effective. Not so with a preacher. Even when he speaks quietly, it will be either in a momentary change of pace, or it will be with a quiet intensity. Loud or soft, slow or fast, if it is preaching, it carries some level of feeling, be it passion, fervor or anxiety.

The late J. C. Massee used to teach homiletics. If a student preacher came across as too low-voltage, Massee was known to reach down into his briefcase, pull out the morning paper, spread it out at arm's length and pointedly read it.

Introduction

There was another teacher who, during a dull sermon, would mount the platform, grip the student by the shoulders and cry into his startled eyes, "Preach! Preach!"

By definition, preaching requires intensity of feeling. This book will attempt to show what rightly enters into that intensity and to show the path to get there. Many books treat the mechanics of preaching; this one will treat those mechanics almost in passing. It will consider them not as means to make a creditable performance, but rather as means to press God's Word upon your hearers and lead them to make spiritual decisions.

Why Preach?

Why should we preach with this urgency of feeling? We preach to represent the Most High God. God called us to do it, and we preach under a divine compulsion. God called Moses from the desert. God called Samuel, and all Israel knew that God had established him to be a prophet. God overwhelmed Isaiah in the temple, and we can hardly call him a volunteer. God set apart Jeremiah from the womb. We read that the hand of the Lord was upon Ezekiel. Jesus summoned all the apostles, and Paul wrote that he was called to be one. Most of us would testify to something of the same, a personal conviction that God wants us to preach His Word. "Now then we are ambassadors for Christ, as though God did beseech you by us: we pray you in Christ's stead, be ye reconciled to God" (2 Cor. 5:20). Little wonder that Paul said necessity was laid upon him. To him preaching was a divine compulsion. Woe if he quit.

More than that, it is the eternal Word of God that we preach. Not all preaching is Scriptural, but we probably agree with Paul that it ought to be. Doubtless we all have heard preaching that seemed a travesty of Biblical preaching. Our concern, however, implies that we hold a common ideal that we ought to preach the Bible. God must be but little impressed when we preach our own ideas. We may tremble at the gravity of our task. If He settled His Word eternally in Heaven, we dare not take it casually. Since He inspired it to the very jots and tittles, we dare not quote it carelessly or preach something that only approximates its doctrines. It carries a fearful duty, but at the same time it carries a high privilege. Can any other task be more important?

More than that, we preach to immortal souls. Their immortality may lose its urgency to us when so many refuse the gospel or when things press in on us. We wonder that so few people give evidence that their immortality concerns them. Yet whether we feel it or not, we know that some of the souls we preach to will eternally find themselves in a joy that goes beyond all imagination. The rest will certainly find themselves in total and endless misery. It may well be true that the gates of Hell are locked on the inside, but locked they are; and our preaching may be the means to keep some souls from ending up behind those gates. How shall they hear without a preacher? We preach because the eternal destiny of souls depends on it.

More than that, we preach the distinctive message of the Cross. Popular theology would have us believe that all religions are one, a notion that Christians flatly reject. In no way can all the various moralizing religions be reconciled with the message of the Cross. The message of the Cross is unique; no other religion takes such a view of human depravity or of man's need for a divine Substitute to die in his place. No other religion reveals God's love as measured by the Cross. No other religion or system can give such hope to sinners. This is the unique gospel that we preach.

More than that, we preach to save lives. Depending on how we preach to them, Christians will rejoice in victory or slog along in defeat. They will live trusting God, or they will live in anxiety and calculation. They will get from God the power of the Holy Spirit, or they will try to serve Him in the energy of the flesh. They will enjoy a clear conscience, or they will carry a load of guilt. Depending on how we preach, they will live in some measure of abundance, or they may never have enough money. For many of them, our preaching will even bear on their health. For families, our preaching can mean a new love and solidarity; or if we fail, some families will fragment, and believers will live in alienation and regret. Preaching carries a fearful responsibility, and we may be at least as responsible if we fail to preach or fail to preach well.

There's more. Preaching is a major part of making a New Testament church go. In a truly liturgical church, the sermon is an incidental part of the Sunday service. In the nonliturgical church, however, the sermon takes the central place in the service; it is even more important than the offering. The very placing of the furniture says it: In most of our churches the pulpit is the prominent piece in the auditorium, the one truly central object, because the preaching of the Word of God is central. Every week people come to that room to hear a fresh word from God. In some

Introduction

churches they may have given up expecting it, but we still have ordered our services on the basis that preaching is central. Our people have some right to expect a message from God, and the Lord has called us to give it to them.

In making a church go, the preaching does more than complete the service. Vital preaching invigorates the whole program of the church; its enthusiasm works its way all through the life of the church. Those who take part in the service draw confidence and fervor from a preacher who has confidence and fervor. Vital preaching inspires the Sunday School teachers. It makes sense of the calling program; is it not easier to invite people to hear a preacher you're proud of? On the other hand, when it's the First Church of Dullsville, the brave, wan smiles of the ushers and teachers reflect the weakness that the pulpit ministry exudes.

We have compelling reasons to preach, and as these reasons become driving concerns, we can hope to achieve some measure of pulpit excellence. God may hear our prayers and reveal Himself through our lips. The fire may then smolder in our bones and flame on our platforms. Bible passages will come to life with a terrible urgency. And men will know that a prophet has been in their midst.

CHAPTER 1

WHAT RIGHT DO YOU HAVE TO SAY THAT?

Confident, passionate preaching rightly flows from the right kind of person. Granted that some preachers can turn on the passion, let us believe that God has a different way for us. Let us believe that honest passion bases itself on things being fundamentally right. That is, the concept of the task is right, and the preacher is right.

The Right Idea of the Task

As we view the preaching task, we should be able to distinguish the popular conception from the Biblical conception. Experience should bear out that the usual view is to regard preaching as a performing art. For years our youth ministries have put on preaching contests, and these contests have drawn little protest. At the same time our Bible schools and seminaries have majored on the mechanics of preaching, making it more of a performance than a ministry or an exercise of a gift. For the last decade the electric church has brought us a galaxy of pulpit stars, in living color and in the setting of show business. Could we not be pardoned for supposing that preaching is a performing art?

I have on my desk two sermon evaluation sheets currently in use at a school of excellent Biblical pedigree. The first sheet is for use in first-year classes, the other for second year. They look typical of such evaluation forms. They each give the grader about thirty points to use as he grades a man's preaching in class. Neither sheet so much as hints at the use of Scripture, at the power of the Holy Spirit, at the precision or completeness of the exegesis or at how closely the outline stays to the text passage. Except for one final note on overall impact, all is mechanics and performance, nuts and bolts. If this shows the thinking of a top school, are we not to think of preaching as a performing art?

I believe that the Bible gives us a different view of the task. The Old Testament prophet got a burden from God by a kind of immediate perception. He then preached it with the words, "Thus saith the Lord."

What Right?

Deuteronomy is loaded with this conception, and so is everything from Isaiah to Malachi. God held men accountable for the way that they listened or neglected to listen to such preaching. He warned Ezekiel that some of his people would come to hear him as though he were putting on a performance.

> And they come unto thee as the people cometh, and they sit before thee as my people, and they hear thy words, but they will not do them: for with their mouth they shew much love, but their heart goeth after their covetousness. And, lo, thou art unto them as a very lovely song of one that hath a pleasant voice, and can play well on an instrument: for they hear thy words, but they do them not. And when this cometh to pass, (lo, it will come,) then shall they know that a prophet hath been among them (Ezek. 33:31–33).

And for such a low concept they brought on themselves the judgment of God.

The New Testament concept of preaching is close to that of the Old Testament. To the world it may be foolishness, but God gets pleasure using it to save men (1 Cor. 1:18–25). According to Romans 10:14–17, God uses preaching to generate saving faith. To the Corinthians Paul wrote that his preaching was not with excellency of speech or of wisdom, but in weakness, fear and much trembling. He added, "And my speech and my preaching was not with enticing words of man's wisdom, but in demonstration of the Spirit and of power" (1 Cor. 2:4). Such preaching can hardly be classed as a performing art; indeed, Paul's language altogether rules out any notion of a performance.

Some other New Testament truths bear on that high concept. The first is the coming of the Holy Spirit. If the Spirit directed the Old Testament prophets, how much more has He become accessible by indwelling New Testament believers? The indwelling presence surely bears on our spoken ministries. At this point we may note that of the four or five passages that list the gifts of the Spirit (Rom. 12; 1 Cor. 12; 14; Eph. 4), none of the lists mentions any form of the word for preach or proclaim. That suggests that mere proclamation is too common an activity to list as a gift. On the other hand, the only term that appears in all the lists is prophecy. So where does that leave us? It leaves us with the impression that prophecy is the most important gift and that it is the sort of preaching that God endorses.

That may take time to accept. Many of us have been brought up to believe that prophecy ended when the last book of the Bible was completed. If prophecy means the miraculous predicting of the future, it apparently did end. However, that is not the way that Paul explained it. In 1 Corinthians 14:1, he made it the one gift to seek. In verse 3 he minimized the miraculous when he said, "But he that prophesieth speaketh unto men to edification, and exhortation, and comfort." That is so important that I am going to repeat it: "He that prophesieth speaketh unto men to edification, and exhortation, and comfort."

To Paul, then, prophecy meant getting the Spirit's help to speak for edification, exhortation and comfort. We may take this as the New Testament idea of preaching—not putting on a performance, but delivering a Spirit-empowered message.

The second New Testament truth bearing on this idea is that the canon is long since complete. We needn't expect revelations; the Spirit brings to remembrance what God has already spoken. Therefore the last chapter that Paul ever wrote told Timothy to preach the Word, to preach what God had already revealed.

In one sense, New Testament preaching is commonplace; we preach the Book. It is our whole stock in trade. We do not nourish people by feeding them our own ideas and opinions. Peter wanted his readers to long for the sincere milk of the Word so that they might grow thereby. We have the Bible, and that's what we are to preach.

But in another sense, Biblical preaching has something of the supernatural about it. Paul ruled out the notion of a performing art when he said that his preaching was in demonstration of the Spirit and power. If we would preach with the fire from off the altar, we would preach on the same basis, trusting God the Spirit to convey Bible truth through our lips. And that concept is a light-year away from supposing that we are putting on a performance, however religious.

Spiritual power may be elusive, but we yearn to have it. We know in our hearts that a knowledge of human nature and group dynamics is a poor substitute for the Spirit's power. Paul had the power of the Spirit when he worked in Corinth, and his two-year ministry there left a large and thriving church (1 Cor. 2:1–4). Later the Judaizers complained that he could show no letters of recommendation. Paul replied that the very existence of the Corinthian church was all the recommendation he needed. The Spirit's power is not the same as enthusiasm or persuasion, but it tends to generate those qualities.

Spiritual power is not in the class of the gifts. The gifts appear to be constant. Read 1 Corinthians 12:12–25, and you get the impression that if the Spirit gives you one of those abilities, you have it for good. Whatever you may believe about miracles, verse 11 says that you have a gift, whatever gift that the Spirit issues you. The next verses say that the gift makes you permanently useful to the body. Use it or neglect it, improve it or not, the gift stays with you. Power is another matter. Some months later, Paul wrote about his thorn. In words that fascinate the expositor, he said, "For this thing I besought the Lord thrice, that it might depart from me. And he said unto me, My grace is sufficient for thee: for my strength is made perfect in weakness. Most gladly therefore will I rather glory in my infirmities, that the power of Christ may rest upon me" (2 Cor. 12:8, 9).

Now note those last words, "That the power of Christ may rest upon me." The word "rest" means temporary residence. That suggests that power is not constant. God may grant it, and He may withdraw it. He grants the power when human nature has quit clutching at glory. So we pray for divine power, and we trust in some way to qualify for it.

To sum it up, when a preacher gets a fresh burden from God and conveys it by expounding Scripture in the power of the Holy Spirit, he is exercising the gift of prophecy. If you have ever heard that sort of preaching, you know when you hear it again, and you have a holy longing to hear more of it. If you are a preacher, you have a holy longing to preach that way yourself every time you preach.

The Right Preacher

Cannoneers once had a maxim that the cannon needed to weigh at least one hundred times as much as the ball to be fired from it. We tend to look on preachers in the same way. The impact of a sermon varies with our respect for the preacher. Let's turn that around: The impact of our preaching varies with our hearers' respect for us. So what do we need to do to earn that respect?

Most of us would agree that we need a call from God. By this we mean a conviction, by whatever means, that God wants us individually and personally in His service. This is the basis of our authority, of our right to stand and proclaim Scripture to men.

That call has become the subject of debate, and in an era of spiritual cooling, little wonder. When divine mandates have become suggestions and preferences, is it any surprise that many should regard God's call to service as nothing more than a preacher's inclination? However, the Scriptural pattern is still on the side of the call as we have long understood it. Moses met God at the burning bush, and for the remaining forty years of his life he seems never to have doubted that God had called him personally. Samuel was destined from before his birth, called in childhood and kept in service to his last. Isaiah saw the Lord high and lifted up, and we find nothing in his writings to show that he ever doubted that God had him for life. Jeremiah wearied of his call and wanted to open an inn; but the fire in his bones would not go out, and God toughened him against his opposers. The Lord called Peter from fishing, and twice Peter went back to the old stand; but the Lord never let him off, and He promised in John 21 that Peter would remain true until death. Paul spoke repeatedly of his call, remarking that a stewardship was entrusted to him, that woe was unto him if he quit preaching the gospel.

With that call comes a certain confidence. People may orate with self-confidence, and some may preach with it. But the confidence we need does not well up from self, nor does it depend on a feeling of self-worth. The confidence that fuels that holy fire is the assurance that God Himself has called the preacher into that situation.

Another quality that people expect in a preacher is diligence. They expect him to have done his homework. David asked if it were thinkable to offer to God that which had cost him nothing. While salvation is by grace, and holy insight comes the same way (James 1:5), the full knowledge of Scripture comes by hard work. In other generations the preacher was, or was expected to be, the intellectual leader of the community. In this century we have largely transferred that duty to the newspaper editor or to any professional man's opinion, however uninformed. Indeed, a strong argument for using careful, standard English is that without it we have little hope of reaching the actual leaders of the community. If the banker or the editor turned up in church, let us hope that he would be likely to come back and not that the language used in the pulpit would turn him off.

This is not to encourage pride of intellect, that Pied Piper who has led so many into spiritual oblivion. It is to encourage diligent study at least in preparation of the sermons we preach. We do not parade our learning, but our hearers will still know if we have mastered the text, learned the background material and reflected long enough to get fresh illustrations. They will sense the difference between easy generalizations and the discreet use of specifics and details.

We know enough people who think we work only three hours a week. We do not need to feed that notion. But the antidote is not in telling about how busy we keep. It comes in showing unobtrusively that in prayer and study, the sermon cost us plenty.

Most would agree that the preacher needs to live a consistent life. To a degree, people will tolerate human frailties. However, glaring problems will turn them off, even if they do not vote us out right away. They expect us to practice what we preach, however irksome this practice can sometimes be to us. They even call us "Reverend," which once meant that we were to be revered. We may sometimes wince at having to bear a word that better applies to God, but it suggests that for many years people have expected us to live up to a certain standard. This standard is not a code that they impose on us; we make the code ourselves. They take the standard that we place upon them. If our people see any appreciable gap between our preaching and our conduct, we will forfeit their respect in direct proportion to the width of that gap.

Can a preacher continue very long without a high level of respect from his hearers? Our experience may well fish up some dramatic cases of scoundrels who survived brilliantly; but we must reject their example. If we cannot live by a given principle, we had better not preach it. The dissonance is bound to hurt our message and cut away at our confidence, or else it will make actors of us; and neither alternative can be tolerable to a messenger of the Cross. We simply must live what we preach.

This consistency is a definite help to urgency. If we have accredited our message by our own experience, we have just that much more reason to preach that message with pulpit fire. The Bible itself is the absolute truth, the Word of God, and it is enough of a reason all by itself for pulpit passion. But when our experience confirms what we have studied, then so much the more can we preach with urgency. Does not our memory bear this out? When God has dealt with us about a matter, say, giving above the tithe, is it not easier to preach generous giving? And will not our increased confidence raise our level of fervency?

Most of us would agree that a preacher needs to be right with God. The late pianist Paderewski gets the credit for saying that if he missed a day of practice, he could tell it. If he missed two days, his close friends could tell it. If he missed three days, his audiences could tell it. The life in the Spirit roughly corresponds to that. In one sense our walk with God is our own business, and we do not parade whatever holiness we may have. We learned long ago that if we preached with known sin unconfessed, we were in trouble. Something would not quite fit. If we let such a condition go on, we will sense that something is wrong, even if we thrust from our minds the desire or the resentment that we are loath to confess.

Recently one of my students gave me a personal example of that principle. Within the past week he had the opportunity to buy a classic sports car. He wrestled with his soul over it; at a time when his wife's shoes were worn out, he would have to borrow the money to buy the treasure. It was at that point that he preached to the class about the nature of God, and all through his sermon he felt a lack of liberty. When class was over, he went back to the video room to review his sermon. In the darkened solitude, he considered the weight that he knew he must lay aside. Before the tape had finished, he resolved to be done with it; it wasn't worth hindering his preaching.

What's more, if we try to preach when something is wrong, some of our hearers will sense it, even if they have no idea of the specifics. At this we are in trouble indeed. The Lord knows the specifics, and so do we.

> Who can understand his errors? Cleanse thou me from secret faults. Keep back thy servant also from presumptuous sins; let them not have dominion over me: then shall I be upright, and I shall be innocent from the great transgression (Ps. 19:12, 13).

On this basis we can trust that the words of our mouth, as well as the meditation of our hearts, may give pleasure to God, conviction to our people and confidence to our own souls. By confessing our sins and by claiming grace we will have accredited our right to preach.

QUESTIONS FOR DISCUSSION

1. What traps can you see in regarding Christianity as a form of show business?

2. What differences can you list between a New Testament sermon and an artistic performance?

21

What Right?

3. What Scriptures deal with the qualifications for spiritual power?

4. How did Paul argue his record as the basis for his right to preach?

5. How important is it that we speak the standard English of the community's leaders?

CHAPTER 2
FINDING THE BURDEN

The prophets had the confidence that they were speaking for God to needy men. If we take this for ourselves, it means that we are speaking more than the truth in general; rather we are speaking a divine truth, a divine message in particular. A vital pulpit ministry makes a promise and generates expectancy; the congregation expects something fresh from God, and rightly so. But how do we get that message? Do we just search back and forth through the Bible to find a passage that intrigues us?

A friend of mine takes the view that it is not so important to find the right passage as it is simply to pick a passage and then to study it exhaustively. After all, the Word of God is infinite. It is living and powerful all by itself, piercing to the dividing asunder of even the finest distinctions, and is a discerner of the thoughts and intents of the heart. The Word by itself has an energizing power (1 Thess. 2:12) and needs only to be pressed on men to gain decisions and eternal fruit. The keys to a good sermon become the faithful exegesis on which we base it and the meditation by which we perfect it.

While there is much to be said for that view, I am not quite satisfied with it, and you might not be satisfied with it either. We have the many examples of the prophets, whose messages came with the words, "Thus saith the Lord." If it be answered that they were writing verbally inspired Scripture, and we are not, true enough. But they still left us a pattern to follow; and we tend to expect something special, something particular when someone speaks for God. I believe that even in this age of grace, when we have finished revelation in the Bible, we still rightly expect some divine nudge, some Holy Spirit guidance to the burden or the passage that we are going to preach. There is still something supernatural about it. If we expect the Holy Spirit to empower us while we preach, we feel easier asking His blessing if we have already asked His message. If we expect Him to move the hearts of our hearers, we can pray with greater liberty if we have already asked Him to move our own hearts. So we ask God what to preach.

We can still trust God for Holy Spirit power. Peter was filled with

Finding the Burden

the Spirit at Pentecost and again when he spoke to the Sanhedrin (Acts 4). Stephen finished his message full of the Holy Ghost (Acts 7:55). Paul urged the Ephesian Christians to pray in the Spirit, "And for me, that utterance may be given unto me, that I may open my mouth boldly, to make known the mystery of the gospel" (Eph. 6:19). Do not all of us long to preach with Holy Spirit power? If we seek the power, can we not also seek the burden itself?

Sometimes He makes it easy. Each of us may think of times when the burden has struck our minds by surprise, perhaps even before we had thought to pray for it. You're driving, cutting the yard or whatever; and the message simply comes to you, probably with the conviction that it came from God. The late Mrs. Robert McQuilkin remarked to me that her husband's messages often came to him while he was shaving.

There would seem to be one important basis for getting the Lord's leading, even in such accidental moments, and that is a regular prayer life. You don't pick up FM programs on an AM radio band, and you can't count on getting shortwave broadcasts without a shortwave receiver. If you have cultivated communion with God by having a regular time alone with Him, you can with some assurance trust Him to show you what He wants you to preach. Everything else in this chapter assumes this foundation.

There may be some other things we need to do in advance. The burdens seem to come when we have already been thinking along those lines, whether on our ministries or on Scripture or on individual needs in our congregation. I think of a preacher, now dead, whom I still admire greatly, and I suspect that a good many of his preaching impulses came negatively, as he leafed through religious magazines and his righteous soul was vexed at the materialism and externalism he found in print. Those wrong values were pressing down on his people. But wherever his initial impulses came from, he preached and wrote like a prophet against the shallowness and fakery of much that passes for Christianity. At the same time, his ministry gave every evidence of an earnest walk with God.

As we ask God for His burden, we actually are asking two distinct answers to our prayer: the burden and the passage that best conveys that burden. We need both. The burden without a passage gives us a topical sermon. The passage without the burden gives us a Bible lesson. The passage with the burden gives us the basis of an expository sermon, conveying the authority of God's Word and phrasing God's claims in the

24

way most likely to bring about resolve and a changed life.

The Sermon Series

What about the sermon series? It certainly lessens the concern two or three times a week to find something fresh, and it carries several other advantages. First, it has continuity, and thereby it offers the hope of giving our people a better understanding of the Bible. A second advantage of preaching a series is that it reduces the occasions for people to accuse us of preaching at them. A capable preacher I know is sensitive about that sort of thing, and in private he has mentioned repeatedly the way that a series can somehow happen on matters that are, in fact, burning in the church. But since the preacher came on the subject as a matter of course, no one has to feel singled out, and the preacher can deal with a given sin or problem with more urgency than he might have felt he could otherwise bring to bear.

Another way of handling the series has a great deal to be said for it. This involves beginning Sunday morning, continuing that evening, then midweek, then morning again, and so on. This approach carries some further advantages. For one, it can increase interest and attendance, especially if we continue the series through the weekly schedule. How much easier it is for us when the evening message treats the next chapter after that of the morning message, and the midweek treats the next chapter yet. It also encourages the morning-only types in our congregations to come back for the evening and midweek services, so as to avoid missing the vitals in the series.

A second advantage is that this full series enables us to concentrate our own attention on a single book or passage at a time. We do not have to divide our concentration between two or even three different subjects a week; and we can hope that our minds will generate more of the insights that give freshness and depth to preaching.

A third advantage is that our series lasts for weeks instead of months. How many congregations have wearied over a sermon series that went just too long? How many preachers have committed themselves to expound Isaiah, feeling they had to do justice to all sixty-six chapters?

But does not preaching a series still require us to get the mind of the Lord? I believe it does, only in not quite the same way. Instead of our having to search for each message we preach, we need to assure ourselves that we have divine direction in the choice of the series.

Intercession

But what if the message still doesn't come? You prayed for it, and God hasn't yet answered. You consulted your recent concerns, including your last shave, and you still don't have the seeds for a sermon. I believe that without presuming on the divine sovereignty you can proceed with some confidence and trust that He is about to give you a fresh burden and perhaps also a passage to go with it. How? Perhaps the best way to open our minds to the Holy Spirit is by interceding for our people. As we pray for them, burdens will come; and can we not trust that those burdens are in some sense carried from the throne room and that they come in terms of Scripture?

If there are cautions in preaching from our intercession, one might be the temptation toward a need-centered or experience-centered ministry. Could we not glide off toward a sort of humanism? The corrective here is that we preach the Bible, even if the divine nudge toward the passage came as we prayed for our people. Another temptation might be to get so specific that our people recognize themselves or one another in the sermon. We can blunder into that quite innocently, and the caution is one that we must keep always before us.

On the other hand, we commonly hear the complaint, "My church is not meeting my needs." We know that sometimes that is only a substitute for more carnal grievances. Yet if we consult our intercession, we might well head off at least some of the occasions for that complaint. We have the examples of the prophets, who did read the spiritual needs of their people. The disgruntled may indeed feel that the church is not meeting their wants, but we have some hope of preaching what they need. As we plead with God for them, we can hope for the divine nudge toward the passage that will truly meet needs, either theirs or at least someone's.

Preaching Our Quiet Time

As we seek what to preach, we face the question as to whether we should preach our quiet time. The stock answer for years has been no, and with good reason. If in our daily devotions we are looking for sermon ideas to meet the needs of others, we can probably find such ideas, but the price will be that we will fail to hear any still, small voice speaking to our own hearts. When we ourselves so badly need the day-by-day renewing of the inner man, we simply cannot afford to lose our quiet time by using it for something else. That is surely as suspect as diverting tithe money—and spiritually as dangerous. I suppose that all of us have heard testimonies that confirm that observation.

With that caution firmly in mind, however, an earnest friend of mine told me that he has begun to preach from what he gets from his quiet time. His reason is that when the Lord has finished dealing with him about a passage, the matter takes on a new reality, a new urgency, which he can then preach with all the greater confidence. I think he is on solid ground, as I trust that he has walked with God long enough not to let sermon preparation interfere with his own perception of the still, small voice. It can be done, and a person who has walked with God should have the spiritual insight to know how to draw on those resources without muddying up the fountain.

In many circles we have drawn the distinction between the prophet and the priest, and we have identified the preacher with the prophet. Alone in his study, a pastor carries on a priestly ministry as he pleads with God for the members of his flock. In the pulpit, however, he becomes a prophet, speaking on behalf of God to men. To carry on that ministry means that he must already have labored with God for the message he is to deliver. Most of us would agree that that takes work. We want the prophets' fire and passion as we preach. But without that work, any fire in our pulpits will hardly trace to the coals on the altar.

QUESTIONS FOR DISCUSSION

1. On what grounds can you believe that God answers prayers for things such as sermon themes?

2. How can you know if He answers?

3. Why does the New Testament say so little about a person's daily quiet time?

4. Just how did the Old Testament prophets get their material?

Finding the Burden

5. In terms of Christian experience, explain what Paul meant by "praying in the Spirit." Does it have anything to do with getting God's leading?

CHAPTER 3

PREACHING IS FOR DECISION

"And if it seem evil unto you to serve the LORD, choose you this day whom ye will serve" (Josh. 24:15).

"As ye know how we exhorted and comforted and charged every one of you, as a father doth his children, that ye would walk worthy of God, who hath called you unto his kingdom and glory (1 Thess. 2:11, 12).

Why preach? To get information across? More than this.

Why preach? To get people to admit the truth of what was said? More than this.

Why preach? To clear our souls and discharge our obligation? To present Scripture in such a way that men will become eternally accountable before God? More than these.

We preach in the hope and with the purpose that men will make decisions, solemn and Scriptural resolves. Whether it be that they trust Christ as Savior or turn from sin or respond to some Biblical entreaty, we preach for decisions.

By definition a sermon is not a Bible lesson. If the purpose of a Bible lesson is to instruct, the purpose of a sermon is to persuade. In a Bible lesson persuasion is secondary; in a sermon the instruction is secondary. A sermon will have content; after you have preached in a place for three months, the people ought to know more than they did before you came. But we should never forget that however much content we offer in our sermons, our preaching is to persuade. We reach our goal in the holy resolves that our people make when they hear us preach. For convenience we may observe the distinction between the sermonic and the didactic—the sermonic to persuade and the didactic to instruct. But is preaching for decision really all that important? It is, and this book recommends that every time we preach, we preach for decision. Even when our battered sheep most need the comfort of the Scriptures, their acceptance of that comfort involves a decision, usually to believe the Lord. Five compelling reasons tell why we ought to preach for decisions.

Reasons to Preach for Decisions

First, the Bible speaks to the will. Jesus said, "If any man will do his will, he shall know of the doctrine, whether it be of God, or whether I speak of myself" (John 7:17). This seems to mean that God did not give His Word to ease our curiosity. He speaks first to the will and to the conscience, and only then to the reason. In obeying the Bible we get understanding of it. This note is so strong in the Old Testament that some have supposed that it taught a salvation by works. Moses spoke to the will. The Poetic Books speak to the heart and to the will, especially in the books of Psalms and Proverbs. The prophets preached repentance; they predicted coming events so as to accredit their right to speak for God. Revelation 1:1 says that God gave the Book to His slaves; no wonder then that the proud get so little out of it. To preach for decision is to conform to the pattern by which God spoke in the whole tenor of Scripture.

Second, the Bible's sermons are sermonic, not didactic. Even the most cursory look at the Bible's sermons ought to confirm that they were after decisions. Deuteronomy fairly throbs with preaching material, and all of it asks Israel to decide. Joshua demanded that they choose that day whom they would serve. Samuel pressed the people to repent of asking a king for themselves. The prophets constantly preached for decisions. John the Baptist, the last of their line, called on Israel to repent; and he baptized those who did. Jesus regularly preached for decisions, and even the discourse in Matthew 5–7 ("And he opened his mouth, and taught them") confronted them with the demands of spiritual holiness.

Consider the ten sermons quoted or summarized in Acts. Seven clearly ask for repentance or conversion, and two more probably would have (Acts 10 and 22) if the preacher had been permitted to continue. The tenth, Paul's address to the Ephesian elders, also calls for decision, this time to faithful service. Ten out of ten.

Third, the sermonic approach is rhetorically sound. If we preach for decision, and just one decision, every time we preach, several benefits ought to present themselves. For one thing, a message prepared on this basis is almost bound to have unity, and unity is a long step toward clarity. Press one divine claim for thirty minutes on a congregation, and nobody will go out wondering what the sermon was about.

Preaching for decision gives purpose to a message. How often has every one of us had the experience of hearing a sermon and then wondering what we were supposed to do? How do we use it? Or weren't we to do anything but merely give our assent? How often have we endured a dull, rambling sermon; and when someone asked us how the preacher did, we could honestly reply that he had preached the truth? We might even have added the word "fearlessly." When many sermons are about as spiritually helpful as a recitation of the multiplication table, small comfort that the truth was preached. They could have preached for decision.

Preaching for decision has the further value of helping grip attention. For many of us, attention is by no means automatic, but a message that makes a clear demand on a person's will has a better chance of gripping interest than a message merely to inform. For most of our congregations, what information can we give them that they haven't heard already?

Spurgeon said somewhere that no one ever went to sleep in a lawyer's office when a will was about to be read, a will in which he expected to get something. No prisoner ever went to sleep in the dock as his sentence was about to be read.

Preaching for decision harmonizes with what we observe about automatic response and transfer of training. Occasionally people may apply our truths even if we do not specifically press them to apply them. Don't count on this happening often. Experiments on transfer of training have dashed many hopes that such a thing does occur. Studying geometry does not much help platform debaters, and chess of itself does not seem to make great military strategists. A pastor told me once that if only he could get his people straight on the National Council of Churches, he thought that they would as a matter of course separate from worldly amusements. Could it be any surprise that his church greatly disappointed him?

Most preachers can tell their own classic stories of how they made the claims of Christ as clear as human language could make them, and yet their hearers seemed to grasp and apply pitifully little of what they had heard preached. We are still accountable to make God's Word clear, and if we forthrightly preach for specific decisions, we have more reason to believe that our hearers will make them. We can hardly hope that our people will drift toward God or that they will somehow become increasingly godly. We have strong reason to believe that people grow spiritually only as they make solemn resolves.

Fourth, the sermonic approach is consistent with spiritual life. Of the objections that some might raise to this chapter, possibly the strongest might be that this whole concept tends to feed the flesh, as though spiritual results come from human effort. Having begun in the Spirit, we are now made perfect by the flesh. Having begun in the Spirit we are now made perfect by making these decisions, that this whole point of preaching for decision boils down to plain legalism, something that Paul wrote Galatians to counteract. This would mean that we are back to preaching dos and don'ts. Perhaps. Do we not hear a great deal of preaching that gives the impression of just such a view?

Since this objection has merit, it is one we need to face. Legalists may indeed preach for decision, but this does not mean that preaching for decision is necessarily legalism. The legalist has a defective theology, something that cannot be repaired simply by changing his homiletics. But however good our theology, does not this decision-oriented approach feed a legalistic mind-set into our hearers, as though by their own strength they are able to achieve spiritual gains? No, we don't have to give this impression. It should be wholly consistent with God's grace to preach a clear response to that grace.

We might begin by reviewing our concept of spiritual life. We might reflect on Romans 8, on 1 Corinthians 2 and 3, on the whole book of Galatians, on Ephesians 4 and 5, and perhaps on Colossians. I believe that preaching for decision will then show itself to be compatible with walking by faith, with communion with God, with the power of Christ's indwelling presence and with the Spirit's work in us. It is compatible with trust, with resting on Christ and with gratitude as the means of realizing victory. Fulfilling any of these involves a resolve, a decision, even if at every point we are cast wholly on God. So we preach for decision even while we guard against any impulse to suppose that we have any sufficiency of our own.

To illustrate this, we need only consider how many spiritual transactions involve a decision; for example, conversion itself. Is there any carnal way to be saved? Of all the ways we can offer salvation—believe on Him, ask Him to save, turn to Him, look and live, invite Him in, repent of your sins—all require a decision, a response. Curiously, even though the Lord phrased the new birth in John 3 in the passive, "Ye must be born again," He still put it in the imperative.

Fifth, preaching for decision is consistent with clear sermon organization. A foundational principle of rhetoric and homiletics is that clarity requires unity. One idea has to rule the whole sermon. We may wonder at the flimsy outlines and the odd digressions that we sometimes hear, which proves the truism that you build a sermon on one controlling idea. Preaching for decision fits this concept. As you study your text passage, you ask what one thing it requires. That is important, and I am going to repeat it: You ask of your text passage what one thing it requires. Except maybe the genealogies, every passage of the Bible makes some sort of demand on the reader. Since a chapter might contain many commands and applications to conduct, the expositor needs to satisfy himself that he has isolated the one demand that controls all the rest. This demand now becomes the proposition for his sermon outline, and it also provides the basis for his statement of purpose.

The Statement of Purpose

Numbers of recent books on preaching have stressed the importance of writing out a statement of purpose. This statement ought to take no more than a sentence. Ideally it goes right on the front of your outline sheet. It spells out in simple terms the change you hope to see in your people as a result of their hearing this sermon. At this point in the century it would appear that much preaching asks only assent; thank God for the rest. If we could set ourselves every time we preach to make out a written objective, it would go a long way to helping our people gain from hearing us.

How are we to evaluate a sermon? By its beauty, Scripturality or homiletical precision? By the polish in its delivery? By the number of responses to the invitation?

Should not the worth of preaching be measured in the congregation? After all, how are we to evaluate a ministry or a campaign of special meetings? Does it not come down to matters such as this: Are the people walking closer to God than they were before the meetings began? Without clear statements of purpose, is it not hoping too much to suppose that our people will be changed for having heard us? Preaching for decision makes it easy to form a statement of purpose, and it provides a means to reach that purpose.

QUESTIONS FOR DISCUSSION

1. Just what is spiritual growth in a believer? To what extent is it

conscious? Or automatic? What can preaching have to do with it?

2. What spiritual applications do you see for Murphy's Law?

3. If you had to debate it, what Biblical case could you construct for or against the idea that people automatically apply Scriptural principles to their conduct?

4. How can we reconcile preaching for decision with the virtues of meekness and gentleness?

5. What does preaching for decision have to do with holy pulpit passion?

CHAPTER 4

CONFIDENCE FROM YOUR EXEGESIS

While this is a book about preaching, not about exegesis, the matter needs to be considered because sound exegesis ought to lead to confident, even passionate preaching. There are Bible expositors out there who are both devoted exegetes and good communicators. However, to listen to a great deal of current preaching might give the idea that preaching and exegesis have little to do with each other. The preacher finds a passage, takes a cursory look at it and then goes on to prepare his sermon. You might read the sermons of the recent past and wonder how many men since Jonathan Edwards did it much differently.

The Puritans' method of sermon organization required the preacher to concentrate on a verse before he undertook to preach it. Their printed sermons often followed this arrangement: The preacher would set out his text, usually a single verse. His first section would list the "Meanings" of the words and of the verse itself. This might take about a page. His second section listed and elaborated the "Doctrines" stated and implied in the verse. This section might take another five pages. His third section was headed "Uses," and here he would explain all of its applications to conduct. These might go on another three or four pages. To us the method may seem a bit didactic, but it suited men whose study day lasted up to eleven hours, and it must have encouraged a great deal of reflection on the Word. It would seem likely that their people learned some Bible. Many of the hearers took notes.

Since the Puritan era, the amount of actual Bible study that has preceded sermon preparation seems to have steadily diminished. Compare printed sermons from, say, the beginning of the railroads to the present time, and the standard sermon outline follows this sentence: "There are three things that we find in this passage." A pattern such as this makes no great demand that the preacher intensively study the passage he is going to preach. Some men have studied hard, but their number has probably been few.

Confidence from Your Exegesis

At this point I am indebted to Walter Kaiser's *Toward an Exegetical Theology*, and his chapter on this matter. He rightly points out that while seminaries have taught both exegesis and homiletics, something got lost in the minds of their students. Somehow between the two disciplines a great gulf is fixed, and of all the work spent in learning Greek and Hebrew and of all the courses in exegesis, little shows up in the pulpit. A few years ago a prominent seminary took a poll of its alumni. After they had been five years in the vineyard, only ten percent of them were still using their Greek. Only two percent were still using their Hebrew.

A former pastor of mine was at a conference with a fellow speaker who had taken about seven years of Hebrew in his various schools. When someone asked him how much his Hebrew helped him, he smiled mischievously and said, "Well, it helps me look up the words in my Hebrew lexicon."

Are we willing to agree that before God we hardly dare preach about Him until we have done a careful exegesis of the Biblical passage at hand? And do we need proof that when we have prepared in this way, we usually enjoy freshness and confidence when we preach it? Do we need proof that it is worth the work, if only we can discipline ourselves to do it? Do we need proof that pulpit fire in some way goes with the confidence we get from faithful exegesis of the passage? Then how do we proceed? Do we even need a discussion of exegetical method?

For an overnight assignment I once asked a class to bring in a set of procedures by which to master a passage of Scripture. One sharp student turned in a page of about thirty steps. It was a beautifully thorough job, but it is hard to imagine the expositor, however diligent, who would follow so complicated a set of procedures, not even the student himself—who has with the passing of the years done unusually faithful service. On the other hand, when a well-known expositor was asked how he prepared, his answer was that after he chooses a passage, he pulls from his shelves every commentary he owns, reads all these and then goes to work on his outline. While perhaps his explanation did not cover all the work that he actually does, even this much might set him apart as unusually studious. Actually, he was already drawing on a lifetime of intensive Bible study, making him ready to expound a passage the moment he opened one of his Bibles. For us, whatever the order that we may follow, most of our study procedures reduce to about four steps. The first of these has to do with the form of the passage.

The Form

To get the form, which is the foundational structure of the passage, you read it over. Legend has it that before G. Campbell Morgan wrote anything on a passage, he read it through fifty times. Some legends say it was a hundred times. After any of us has read a passage through anything like that many times, he is bound to see the structure of that passage. The natural sequences and divisions in the passage ought to show up clearly.

Now to take an example, notice this conference sermon on 2 Corinthians 5. The theme was the Christian life, and this chapter says three things about it.

The main heads were these:

I. The Walk of Faith (v. 7)
II. The Love of Christ (v. 14)
III. The Vital Witness (v. 20)

To compare an outline like this with the chapter from which it came, it is hard to avoid the idea that the preacher had made no real attempt to understand the passage. It must have seemed less work simply to lift three intriguing phrases and to go to whatever they might suggest. He gave no hint of the real message of 2 Corinthians 5.

Serious exegesis asks what the whole passage means, and the vital first step is to see it as a passage and make a provisional answer to that question. You might well outline the passage. You will probably also be making notes, lists, underscores and question marks.

The Words

A second step of earnest study is to get the very words of the passage. If you can sight-read the original text, so much the better. Riches lie right there on the surface, even before you open your lexicon, as you notice the obvious vocabulary words or compare words you know with their synonyms.

For the words you don't know, there are ways to get them. By reading an alternate translation you can get a better idea of the pivotal words in the passage. Precision, however, requires another route; and it is then no great task to check those words in a major concordance, such as Young's or Strong's. From that point it is possible to look them up in a lexicon. The man who never had Greek can learn the Greek alphabet in an hour, and with this he should be able to figure out enough of a Greek word to look it up in Thayer or Arndt and Gingrich. Hebrew takes a little longer, but even here two hours should give him the alphabet. This will put him in a position to figure out a Hebrew spelling by looking the word up in a concordance and then to make practical use of a lexicon. Of the Hebrew lexicons available, Gesenius' is standard, but Brown, Driver and Briggs gives more information; and it has the advantage of the *Index,* by Einspach, which gives just about every pivotal word in the Old Testament and shows where in B.D.B. to find it. While these books will not give much help on the nuances of constructions, they will give a good idea of the meaning of a given word. And there is gold to be had.

If studying the form of a passage is like using a wide-angle lens, word studies are like using a microscope. Somewhere between the two, however, is locating in the sentence the stressed word. Commonly the stressed word comes first or last in its clause. For example, the stressed word in Colossians 2:3 comes at the end: "In whom are all the treasures of wisdom and knowledge—hidden." Repeating a word may give it stress, as in Romans 10:9, where stress falls on the words "mouth" and "heart." Or a particularly strong word may convey stress, as in 2 Peter 3:9, where "Not willing that any should perish" involves the strong word "Not determining that any should perish."

Setting

A third area to study is the setting of the passage. This suggests two separate considerations, and both need attention.

First, we have to look at the situation of the passage. Of all the concerns of special introduction, we do well to remind ourselves of authorship, speaker, date, place of writing, addressees, situation of addressees and purpose. The historical situation bears on the passage, and our preaching will be the richer for our habitually checking out these wider considerations, even if we do not often mention these findings in our sermons. Some commentaries and Bible histories, however, do attempt to give the historical setting of a given book or event. Checking place names in a Bible atlas is another way of getting Biblically rich.

Then we have to look at the immediate context, by looking back a few chapters and then looking forward a few. We seem to hear many sermons on 2 Corinthians, but except for the two chapters on giving, most of these sermons are on single verses. But how often, or how rarely, do we hear the total message of the book? Or how the letters of commendation in 3:1 and 2 were an irritation that Paul continued to allude to the rest of the way through the epistle? Your own mind will bring up similar examples. Doubtless we all yearn that our people know the Book. We fulfill this yearning, in part at least, by just such disciplines as knowing the total message of each book.

The Commentaries

Mark Twain somewhere described a classic as a book everybody wants to have read but nobody wants to read. This seems to be a widespread ministerial view of the reference books and commentaries. Many of us cover our walls with these sets, at untold cost to our wives, but we may wonder how many of us in our busy ministries have time to read from them.

While a minority may feel that using commentaries is not quite spiritual, most of us would likely agree that there is wisdom to be gained in using them. Most of us would not hesitate to discuss a verse with a friend or a fellow pastor. To discuss the verse with Keil and Delitsch, with Lange or with Ellicott, should be at least as innocent and as helpful. The commentaries contain the collected wisdom of the past and a vast amount of Biblical research. To neglect the books is to impoverish ourselves as well as those who hear us.

After these steps, whatever the order in which we take them, we should have a pretty fair idea of what the Lord is saying here and a far better idea than we had before we began the study process. If our commission is to preach the Word, we can hardly fulfill it without truly studying the Word, and these four general steps ought to help us do just that. A fifth step still awaits us, however, and it takes time.

A truism that students begin to grasp late in their programs is that cramming during the hours before an exam turns out to be temporary and flimsy learning. But if you cram two or three nights before the exam just at bedtime, and then do light reviews from then on, you get much better results, and what you learn stays with you longer. The mind needs time to work on it. The same principle holds in the rest of your study life. Your mind needs time to absorb. If after your exegesis, whether before or during your actual sermon preparation, you have time to reflect, you should gain more from your study. Problem passages tend to open out. Fresh insights occur to you. You see new relationships. But just as you cannot hurry the process of sweeping dust across the floor, you cannot much hurry the process of reflection.

Now back to the point of the chapter. The problem we face is how to make ourselves do the specific Bible study that Bible exposition requires. If we have a problem linking our exegesis to our preaching, we may be either lazy or too busy, or we may never have gotten the habit. Not many schools teach a true method of expository sermon preparation, and few other methods than this or real textual preaching require exegesis. Since it is possible to produce expository outlines after only cursory study of the passage, why go to all that extra work?

I have a volume of sermons preached at the founding of the World's Christian Fundamentals Association, sermons by the finest preachers W. B. Riley could assemble in 1919. The second address uses the text of Luke 18:1, "Men ought always to pray," and gives the English derivation of the word "ought." But the Greek says something different, and it looks as if the preacher never opened his Greek Testament in the process of putting his sermon together. Never mind that he had some good illustrations; we had a right to expect more of him. And we must expect more of our own study. Without genuine and faithful study of the passage, preaching moves toward becoming a performance. With quality study, we can expect more of that passion for which we long.

QUESTIONS FOR DISCUSSION

1. Along with the general steps of exegesis recommended in this chapter, what other steps have you personally found to be helpful?

2. If exegesis is detective work, just how do you go about solving a problem passage?

3. Which commentaries have you found most satisfactory to your own taste? How can you keep from wasting money on the next set that you buy?

4. Why should we work so hard to master the sense of a given passage of Scripture when it has to be the Holy Spirit Who illuminates the Word to hearts anyway?

5. What actual connection do you see between confident mastery of the passage and confident liberty as you preach?

CHAPTER 5

CONFIDENCE IN YOUR ORGANIZATION

What connection can there be between pulpit fire and sermon organization? Is there not among us a common notion that either one of them will hinder the other and that the man who prepared systematically is just not quite sanctified? Do we not hear preachers say almost boastfully, "Now this may not be very homiletical," as though there were virtue in sermonic free flight, unencumbered by the trammels of order? Does real liberty in preaching come from ignoring principles of orderly thinking and communication? Surely not.

Rather than that, good homiletics is the basis of honest, passionate preaching. Good order in preparing gives the more confidence in preaching. When a preacher knows that his logic is shaky or his exposition does not quite fit the text, he may force his passion so as to cover the gap. In effect, however, his unjustified emotion answers to the strange fire that Nadab and Abihu offered before the Lord. Orderly sermon organization is a vital part of all that goes together to make clear, passionate discourse.

If that connection is important, another concern follows it. How do we prove the rightness of homiletic rules? Rhetorical principles may seem right with observation, but they are hard to prove. Someone wrote somewhere that while a mapmaker needs only four colors, it is, or was then, considered impossible to prove it mathematically. Now in our case, how can we set about to prove that an organized sermon is better than a homily? Can anyone prove that a vertebrate is happier than an amoeba? Yet observation must surely tell us that a unit of thought as large as a sermon is far easier to understand if it has arrangement, orderly and symmetrical divisions and progress toward a conclusion. How can we prove that a sermon needs to be divided into main heads? Does it help to use the analogy of the apple—hard to eat one in only one bite? How can we prove the principle of unity, that the whole sermon should be built around one idea or one holy demand? Have we heard enough pulpit hash to convince us that one idea must govern the whole sermon or else it will lose clarity and impact?

Are the Bible's sermons outlined? In many cases they probably are, as for example Paul's address to the Ephesian elders (Acts 20:17–35), which shows a step-by-step progression. The Sermon on the Mount also moves in such orderly sequence as to suggest systematic thought, even if we have a hard time imagining that the Lord used outlined notes. That generalization is hard to affirm or deny, for in few cases, Old Testament or New, can we be sure that we have the whole sermon verbatim. Acts 10 may give Peter's sermon in full to the point at which he was interrupted. Stephen's sermon in Acts 7 looks complete, whether Luke quoted it in full or in summary; Stephen apparently built it on three key rejections (vv. 9, 27 and 39) leading to the ultimate rejection in his conclusion (vv. 51–53).

How then do we proceed to get an outline? We all have had the experience of looking at a chapter, knowing there is a sermon in it but being baffled as to how to get it out. This chapter will give you four simple steps by which you can get it out. These steps really work.

So now what?

Step 1: One Demand

A fundamental principle is unity: What one thing does it say? What one thing? If we accept that the Bible speaks to the will and to the conscience, what one thing does the passage require? If you look at the passage long enough, you will see one truth, one governing idea that embraces everything else. You have to start with this.

Occasionally a sequence of ideas in the passage leaps out at you and tempts you to use them as the main divisions. Yield not to temptation; try to hold them in your mental file until you can find the controlling idea in the passage. I believe that your experience will bear out that if you begin with the main heads and then try to find a unifying principle, something is going to have to be forced into place. Granting that the natural impulse is to fall back on something like "We find three things in this chapter," there is a stronger way to base your message. Is the precision worth all that work? It is if you believe in clarity, rhetorical impact and honest fervency. So you begin with the one decision that the passage demands; any other way leads to the fogs.

In the military museum of the Invalides in Paris is a memorable relic of the Napoleonic wars. It is a polished brass breastplate, apparently taken from the body of a dead horseman. The man must have died of a single cannonball through the middle of his chest. I believe that the effect of a vital, unified sermon on a rebellious human heart might be in some way similar. We do not much help people by giving a scattering of exhortations, as though we were pelting them with handfuls of gravel. We help them when we press a single Biblical demand on them and persuade them at that point to submit to the Lord.

But why not simply proclaim the truth? Does every sermon have to press for a decision? To repeat the point of the opening chapters of this book, (1) a sermon is something other than a Bible lecture, and (2) people do not often apply truths to their conduct, even though we can all testify to those times when the Holy Spirit used some offhand remark to pierce a heart or to heal a wound. Even if for variety's sake we sometimes preach a truism rather than a decision, the sermonic approach is stronger and, I believe, nearer the heartbeat of Scripture. The sermonic approach makes the better norm. When in years past I have for variety delivered a homily rather than an organized sermon, I always came away feeling that I had not fed my people especially well, however many morsels I had offered them.

When you have isolated the one decision stated or implied in the passage, you phrase it into a proposition. The proposition is that key sentence around which you build the rest of your sermon. Ideally it is simple; it contains only three necessary elements: (1) a subject naming the ones to whom the passage applies (you, we, every believer, all men), (2) a should-word (should, must, ought) and (3) an action verb embodying the decision the passage demands. You then add enough words to make a smooth sentence out of it.

The proposition then turns out to be deceptively simple. It adds no qualifications, no explanations, no subordinate clauses—just a simple sentence. In the outline it is a declarative sentence, not a command or a question. It should be perfectly clear or easily explained, and it needs to be free from figurative language. Some reflection ought to bring up the rhetorical reasons for all these criteria. Now for examples, compare these three sentences with their counterparts in the second group:

Every soul should delight itself in fatness.

Believe and obey the Lord to be saved.

Peace can be had by those who will trust.

Now compare those with the following ones:

We ought to enjoy God.

You must take God at His Word.

Every one of us should rest on Christ.

Furthermore, we need to phrase the proposition with force. By this I mean that the proposition should have an action verb rather than a state-of-being verb. How do we prove that one is stronger than the other? Was it Strunk who remarked that the verb "to be" is a colorless glue to join two ideas together? Second, the proposition should use the active voice rather than the passive. Again, how do you prove it? After all, you find passives in the Bible. True. But as you examine writing that you like, you will probably find that the fewer passives in it, the more readable and often the less obscure. When you write in the active voice, the subject performs the action of the verb. We tend to chafe at sentences beginning with "It has been said that—" because we like to know who said it. Put it in the active, and the obscurities vanish. What holds true of our prose in general certainly applies to our propositions in particular.

To get force in phrasing, a third caution is that we put it in the affirmative, not the negative. If we are preaching for decision, a little reflection ought to verify this one. For example, try these:

We ought not doubt God. As against: We must take God at His Word. Or,

A Christian should not sin against the Lord. As against: A Christian should deal with the sin in his life.

The difference may not seem great, but in terms of rhetorical force the affirmative turns out to be much stronger than the negative and much more useful to us.

As a final check on the proposition, we might do well to ask two questions of it. (1) Is it truly Scriptural? In practice, as we work at clear phrasing, we may find ourselves shading away from the actual thrust of the passage. If our people cannot easily sense that the proposition fits the passage—and the discerning ones will sense when we have passed off a contrivance on them—we lose something. (2) Is it spiritually important? This may not be so easy to answer, but the Bible-loving servant of God should be able to make a discerning judgment. So much preaching is simply trivial, and preachers labor to demonstrate what their people already believe. This is not to call the plan of salvation trivial, because certain basic themes such as the Cross, justification by faith and the blood atonement probably need more elaboration than we give them. But when it comes to exemplifying love in our lives or keeping on keeping on or cultivating a good self-image, do we need to say much more? A friend of mine once told me that he had spent six solid months proving that Jesus is the Son of God. I still wonder if he needed all that time. We still need to ask, Is it spiritually important? Do our people need other themes more?

Step 2: The Preliminary Worksheet

So you have a good proposition. Where do you go from here? It may be that a preachable set of main heads has fairly leaped off the page at you. If not, here is a procedure that will work.

Take a sheet of scratch paper and write your proposition across the top. Now ask yourself, If someone were to press that demand on me, what questions would most naturally snap into my mind? Why? How? Any others? Possibly when? or where? Now make a vertical column for every interrogative you want to try. If "Why?" heads your first column, go through the passage you have exegeted and list every possible consideration that tells us why we should obey your proposition. Take your time. Now go on to the "How?" column and put down everything that tends to tell how to fulfill the proposition's demand. If you have other interrogatives, follow the same procedure for them.

Why?	How?	Where?	When?	To What Extent?

Step 3: The Main Heads

Now look at your lists. One of them ought to offer the homiletical raw material for a good set of main divisions. With your Bible and your exegesis notes open in front of you, begin to phrase out a good set of main divisions. Ideally they should fit the natural divisions in the passage. Taken together, they should cover the whole passage without overlapping one another. This is so important that it bears repeating: The main heads do not overlap, and it will usually take work to phrase them in such a way that they are truly distinct. At the same time they should be parallel

Confidence in Your Organization

in form. With a little reflection, these principles of outlining should seem self-evident, but I suspect that few of our schools teach them, despite all the outlines they assign. At the college and graduate level, even sermon outlines do not often have to follow such principles.

Before I go on, let me suggest that the above principles deserve serious reflection. A sermon outline should help people to understand a given passage of Scripture. If we do it right, the outline will be so clear that when we preach it, our people will feel that they might have found the same ideas themselves. We will find ourselves toiling to choose the few words that fulfill our purpose. We may find ways to excuse some hazy language elsewhere in a sermon, but the proposition and main heads need to be cut to fine tolerances. My nephew once remarked in a discussion of billiards that close counts only in horseshoes and hand grenades. In some circles, alas, we might add the word homiletics.

To go on about the main heads, we do well to phrase them with the maximum of rhetorical force. That is, like the proposition, the heads need action verbs in the active voice. The affirmative works harder than the negative. If a main head has no verb in it, we can go on the working basis that it isn't ready yet.

Note that the interrogative leads naturally to the heads. Suppose that the proposition is something like, "We should meet God in prayer daily." If your interrogative is "Why?" you are neatly in line for a series of reasons, each beginning with the word "Because" or a series of results, each beginning with the words "In order to." If the interrogative were "How?" the heads would probably be a series of steps, or ways, each beginning with the word "By," followed by such a participle as preparing, kneeling, praising, confessing—but in any case, verbs.

This is the point at which to consider making a transitional sentence. To go on with the above example, let us suppose a sermon on Luke 11:1–13, with such a proposition as "We should meet God in prayer daily." If the interrogative should be "Why?" the next sentence might well be, "Jesus here gives us several reasons why we should meet Him daily." Note first that this leads directly into the first main head. Note secondly that the word "reasons," the key word, characterizes each of the main heads to follow. The key word becomes your most useful device for keeping the main heads parallel.

A caution here is in order. Watch out for any main head that begins with the words "Because of." Note that it points toward a meaning, but it doesn't state it. For example, compare these phrasings: "Because of Jesus' command" with "Because Jesus commanded us to pray." The second one fulfills what the first one can only promise.

But, really, is precise phrasing all that important? Just because we expect precision in surgery, in dentistry, in technology, in car repair, even in our haircuts, can we not be content with easy approximations in our sermon preparation? Is it necessary to put divine truth into such carefully worded simplicities? Do not the deep truths of the spiritual life come in complicated phrasings, and do we not have to trust the Spirit to apply what we preach? If anyone of us thinks so, let him try making up a simple written test on what he has lately preached and have a few trusted members take it. This ought to persuade any of us to preach clarities, and these begin with clear, precise outlining.

How about alliteration? In most of our circles, alliteration is as important as wearing a tie and shoes at formal occasions. But what good are all those words beginning with the same letter? Rarely does an alliterated series fall easily into place. You have to force the last one in. And why bother? Logical precision is more important, and as a memory key, a series of C's or P's is not all that much help to us, and even less to our congregations. A few hearers may seem impressed, but not so impressed as preachers, and I fear that they get little help from our penchant. Indeed, does not alliteration encourage the notion that imprecisions are all right, that it is innocent to play word games with the Bible and that our contrivances need only approximate the truth? We may be paying high hidden charges for the habit. I believe that the long-term mischief here has been more serious than we might notice. In fundamentalist circles, Biblical inerrancy has been a leading issue, on a par with verbal inspiration, the Virgin Birth and the blood atonement. The fashion of alliteration, however, has encouraged a subtle countercurrent, an impulse to make a given passage say what it needs to say to make the alliterated pattern work out. We may wonder if this may in some way connect with the widespread disregard for the original languages of Scripture.

After we have decided on the phrasing, how many divisions do we need? We need at least two, or we have not divided it. More than five we cannot remember, and certainly our people will not remember more than five. In most of our outlining, sermonic and otherwise, almost any group of more than five coordinates can better be arranged in groups of five or fewer. The Ten Commandments are more easily memorized as two groups of five each, probably the way Moses understood them. The seventeen works of the flesh, in Galatians 5, fall easily into four groups. The fruit of the Spirit arranges easily into three groups of three. Complicated processes become understandable when we arrange long lists into groups of five or fewer. Hence in our outlining, we need at least two main heads and not more than five. Within these limits, fewer divisions are clearer than more.

Step 4: The Final Worksheet

Now that you have a good basic outline, you are ready to begin your final worksheet. Here you do well to get your whole sermon on one side of a sheet of paper. If you letter small, you can do it, and you gain the advantage of being able to see your whole sermon at one look. So leave space for an introduction, and perhaps two inches from the top of the sheet print your proposition. Put in your interrogative, and then spell out a transitional sentence. Your proposition is the last numbered sentence of the introduction.

Right under the proposition put your first main head, leading with the Roman numeral I and closing with parentheses around the verse numbers that your first main head covers. Now do some measuring with your eye. Space the rest of the main heads down the page in such a way that each has an equal amount of space in which you can develop it and still leave some room for a conclusion. In this way you have given yourself the best possible arrangement to help you get the final outline in your mind. You also have a working framework in which you can arrange all the rest of your ideas, insights, cross-references and illustrations. If you letter small and abbreviate, you should have room to set down as much as an hour's preaching material. In an upper corner, letter in your statement of purpose.

Someone asked George Muller how long he prayed. He said, "I pray until I've prayed." In sermon preparation, you prepare until you've prepared. With your worksheet at this stage, you are ready to add material until your sermon is complete. Subheads go in now. Memorable sentences go in, but you will do well to abbreviate them as much as you can. As you come up with illustrations—more on these later—two words ought to be enough of a cue, and since you usually want them at a glance, it makes sense to put each cue in a box. This way you know how many you have and where they are. Get your introduction and conclusion. Put a good title at the top, with your text-passage right under it. When your preparation is finished, you will know it at a glance.

QUESTIONS FOR DISCUSSION

1. Why does preaching compare more closely to band music than to a symphony?

2. Is there any way to prove that a good outline is so important?

3. Why should we labor for homiletical precision, when the hearers seem to remember little besides the illustrations?

4. Why should each main head last about as long as the other main heads?

5. List the criteria for the proposition and think through the reasons behind each one.

6. List the criteria of the main heads and think through the reasons behind each one.

CHAPTER 6

CLEAR MOTIVES

"No man can serve two masters . . ." (Matt. 6:24).

". . . The simplicity that is in Christ" (2 Cor. 11:3).

One of the most neglected aspects in homiletics is an issue that bears subtly on our pulpit impact; that is our impulse to live by more than one set of desires. We preach dedication of lives to the Lord, and we sing such hymns as "I Surrender All," when our own situations may not be all that simple. Indeed, the New Testament word for sincerity may just as well be rendered with such words as "singleness," "simplicity" or sometimes "generosity," virtues that the Bible praises. Whatever complexity there may be in our thinking, our desires have to be single: one face, one ruling passion, one Lord.

God put most of us through a moment of crisis in which we cast ourselves on Him, in what we thought was a final surrender of will, of body, of hopes. This may have coincided with our call to the ministry, but that is another matter. We said no to the flesh and to self, and we resolved to live for God. The words rang in our ears that the world has yet to see what God can do with a man totally dedicated to His will. "If any man will come after me, let him deny himself, and take up his cross daily, and follow me" (Luke 9:23). "I am crucified with Christ: nevertheless I live; yet not I, but Christ liveth in me: and the life which I now live in the flesh I live by the faith of the Son of God, who loved me, and gave himself for me" (Gal. 2:20). So with shining eyes, with determination or resignation, we yielded all to Him and resolved to live for Him.

Then things began to get interesting. What we had thought to be an unconditional surrender began to look more and more like a promissory note. God began to touch sore spots, the reservations we had not realized were there. Old resentments, like underground springs, came to the surface. Someone's rudeness got us to return some rudeness or else to simmer over it. Any moment of triumph ended in a temptation. Whatever it was that was nailed to the cross, something was still writhing and insisting on its own way. We had renounced self, and God had pronounced it dead; but a battle was now going on that in some ways was worse than before the surrender that was to end all the battles.

Clear Motives

The Gulf Stream moves across the Atlantic Ocean at a speed of about three knots. Deep down near the ocean floor another current moves in the opposite direction. As with human activity, what appears on the surface is not necessarily the whole story.

We live with at least two sets of desires. On the one hand, every believer somehow, somewhere within him, wants to live for Christ and to please Him. On the other hand, every one of us lives with a complex of opposite desires wanting to please the flesh. If anyone should suppose that these opposite desires have been done away, he must in all candor admit that the righteous are scarcely saved and that these desires are under only tenuous control. If he supposes that his own former desires are eradicated or controlled, he has only to consult the lives of his denominational colleagues to see how tenuous a control others have over those desires that oppose the yearning to please God.

If God has reckoned to us an absolute righteousness, and if we have the indwelling presence of the Holy Spirit, we can hope for at least a sort of victory over the flesh. There is such a thing as confessing all known sin, even as we cast ourselves at the foot of the cross, praying, "Who can understand his errors? Search me, O God." There is such a thing as examining our motives and judging them, to the point where without any self-congratulation we can trust that our motives are relatively pure.

Once the late Dr. Walter Hughes lectured to a history class I was teaching. I happened to know that during the turbulent 1920s he had built a struggling Toronto church up to a membership of approximately 700 in about four years. When the time came for questions, I asked him how he accounted for the growth of his and other churches during a period of such conflict between fundamentalists and modernists. His answer sticks in my memory: "I think God blessed us because our motives were pure in those days." Doubtless there was experiential truth in what he said, with all due allowance for human frailty. There can be such a thing as acting with unmixed motives.

Why must we keep on cleansing our desires? Personally, because the flesh is so much with us, and homiletically, because mixed desires and mixed motives will reveal themselves in a false note that the discerning will hear. This statement ought to be self-evident, and it would seem that any reader of this chapter will be able to find examples in his own experience. To preach with mixed motives is to be a hypocrite, a phony (1 Thess. 2:3–6). While motive has homiletical implications, the subject does not seem to come up often in seminary chapels, preaching classes or textbooks. Yet of all the many things we need to do if we are to preach with fire, cleansing our motives has to be near the top of the list.

Outright Sins

From Screwtape's point of view, these are the old standbys that the powers of darkness can use to corrupt our messages: the lust of the flesh, the lust of the eyes and the pride of life. How many times in all confidence have we heard credible reports of the pastor who left the bedside of his dying wife to seek comfort in other arms across town, reports we wish never came to our ears? How many confessions of ministerial greed, of hands in the petty cash, of pastors whose life purpose seems to be to shear the sheep? A pastor boasted to a friend of mine that he worked at cultivating the elderly, and he had induced several to will their estates to him personally. By such means he claimed to have put himself in line for bequests totaling well over eight hundred thousand dollars.

Or power, the cold satisfaction in controlling other people, whether on the platform or from a desk? The Son of Man came not to be ministered to but to minister, and Peter cautioned us against lording it over God's heritage (1 Pet. 5:3). Why should the temptation be so powerful? Partly because it seems to catch a man unawares. He is surprised to realize that he has power over others. In what pastors' meeting or chapel did he ever hear a sermon warning him against the pride of life, especially the pride in controlling others' lives?

Or envy. It may be the rottenness of the bones (Prov. 14:30) and the motive for crucifying Christ (Matt. 27:18), but it can still be enormously comfortable to the flesh. Whether it wants the possession that someone else has or the honored position, envy divides the mind and clouds the conscience. This, too, is a sin that seems to get little attention in the pulpit. This is surprising, when we consider how common it is to harbor envy, how corrosive it is to the soul and how dangerous it is to a person's communion with the Lord.

Or resentment. In the care of souls we can make all sorts of mistakes and wound many feelings. In turn as the servants of God we have to accept all manner of slights and injuries, often from people who seem to feel that, after all, the pastor and his wife are strong and ought to be able to take it. Despite all the warnings in both Testaments, for the flesh it is hard to forgive and easy to resent. Yet Paul wrote, "Let all bitterness, and wrath, and anger, and clamour, and evil speaking, be put away from you, with all malice [all resentment]: And be ye kind one to another, tenderhearted, forgiving one another, even as God for Christ's sake hath forgiven you" (Eph. 4:31, 32).

All these sins are hard to hide and dangerous to the souls of many, including our own. We are to lead our people to victory over known sin. To betray this trust by cherishing our own sins is a preaching failure of the worst kind.

The Private Games

Another set of contrary motives are matters that in anyone else might be innocent. Paul wrote to Timothy, "No man that warreth entangleth himself with the affairs of this life; that he may please him who hath chosen him to be a soldier" (2 Tim. 2:4). This means that the ministry demands a single-minded dedication to the Lord—and in a real sense to the institution He puts us in. While the Lord ordained that those who preach the gospel should live of the gospel (1 Cor. 9:14), we accept the principle with the understanding that at some points in our ministry we may have to make tents. The part-time job may be necessary, and we begrudge the time away from the desk and the family. Similarly our chores, hobbies and vacations are to some extent necessities, and we accept them gratefully but with a certain caution.

A woman remarked that she had owned fifty cats. Her husband put in, "On the contrary, my dear, would it not be better to say that fifty cats have owned you?" Not very kind, but it distinguished what counts here. Is the ministry first with us? Or are we really committed to some private game on the side? Some preachers own golf clubs; some golf clubs own the preacher. Some preachers own houses. Sometimes the house owns the preacher. One justified his real estate manipulations by saying that he gave the church eight hours a day, and that the rest of his time was his own. Any wonder that his ministry soon went on the rocks?

The possibilities here seem endless. We probably all know of preachers who have become wealthy by astutely putting money into stocks or real estate—and did many of these avoid spiritual loss to their ministries? A dear friend once told me that he had finally gotten loose from a drug addiction. While he was convinced that it had been a secret between himself and the Lord, he knew his ministry had been powerless for years because of it. Can we think of a hobby more innocent than amateur radio? Yet I once knew of a missionary whose ham radio chitchat was widely believed to come first, that his missionary work could have whatever energies were left over.

No man that warreth entangleth himself with the affairs of this life; but we preachers are constantly in danger of just this, of permitting hobbies and possessions to own us. A legendary preacher in Michigan was known to be willing to serve only such churches as were near good fishing. These things may be innocent in themselves and to anyone else relatively harmless. To someone called to be a full-time soldier of the Cross, however, Scripture requires a single-minded commitment to giving others the Word of God. According to Acts 6, even administrative work may be suspect. Prudential reasons tend to justify our diversions, our acts of mercy and our vacations. The flesh has its ways of finding its own prerequisites and advantages in a situation, and these can easily begin to control our decisions.

And some of the holy fire will go out of our preaching. Perhaps more than just some of it.

QUESTIONS FOR DISCUSSION

1. Why historically have the majority of the churches accepted the principle of a full-time, vocational ministry? Does the abuse of this into sacerdotalism and professionalism negate the principle?

2. To what extent does Paul's tent-making argue against the theme of this chapter?

3. Can our motives ever be really pure?

CHAPTER 7

ILLUSTRATIONS THAT BURN

"And with many such parables spake he the word unto them, as they were able to hear it. But without a parable spake he not unto them: and when they were alone, he expounded all things to his disciples" (Mark 4:33, 34).

Young preachers sometimes have their problems, but probably the most common is that they do not use enough illustrations. In fact, some preachers use almost no illustrations at all; and then they wonder why their people are so blank during the sermon and so perfunctory at the door. The opposite extreme, the pattern of certain successful evangelists, is the sermon that consists of only three or four extended illustrations and then an invitation. This sort of sermon may not have much Biblical content, but at least nobody goes to sleep. The expositor's problem—your problem—is how to preach the Bible in such a way that your people stay awake and learn the Bible. Much of the solution to this lies in the illustrations that you use.

Your illustrations are the most memorable parts of your sermon. If you use an old outline again, some people might notice, probably from marginal notes in their Bibles. If you repeat an illustration, almost everybody will notice. Since illustrations are preaching materials that you use up fast, they are going to take work. And they are worth the work.

At first glance, we might question what illustrations have to do with passionate discourse, with pulpit fire. In one way, not much. Good illustrations can work well without any intensity of delivery. However, they add so much to the preacher's confidence in his message that they tend to increase the fire, and a lack of them tends to damp down the fire. For this reason we cannot afford to neglect the quest for good ones.

Values of Illustrations

A first value is to clarify. If the Lord intended some of the parables to mystify and intrigue the crowds, even those of Matthew 13 left the disciples with a clearer perception of gospel advance and resistance against it than an explanation could have given them.

How do you make it clear to a quibbler that the next person along is the neighbor whom God commands him to love? Say it. Tell him again. Does he get it? Maybe. But tell him the story of the good Samaritan, and you demolish his quibble.

How was Jesus to show the mocking elders that their plot on His life would bring eternal vengeance on themselves and on Israel? He could have affirmed it, and they might have understood. But He told the story of the wicked husbandmen (Matt. 21:33–40). When He put the final question to them, He got the right answer: "He will miserably destroy those wicked men, and will let out his vineyard unto other husbandmen, which shall render him the fruits in their seasons" (v. 41). When He repeated their answer, some of them exclaimed, "God forbid" (Luke 20:16). They had gotten the point of it, all right.

A second value of the illustration is close to the first—to make a truth vivid, or to make someone feel the force of that truth. For example, you're facing a skeptical crowd of people who think that they are holy. If you try to tell them that they are out of harmony with the heart of the God they profess, will they feel their alienation from Him? Unlikely. But suppose you try another approach: Tell them a story that they can identify with. Tell them about the smart son who leaves home and blows his inheritance. Build it up. Show the father's feelings and then his joy at getting his lost son back. Then focus on the older brother, the good boy. He never took a smoke or a beer. He still has the first dollar he ever earned. Cold, selfish, heartless, he is totally out of sympathy with the feelings of his father. If the scoffers can't feel this one, you can be sure that the bystanders will.

Barnhouse told of a wealthy woman who once lived near Philadelphia. She was known as Mrs. Mack. She taught a Sunday School class of teenage girls. One day her chauffeur stopped at the home of one of her girls and left a large florist's box. When the girl opened it, she found a number of overage roses, petals falling, leaves withered. Mystified, she guessed that the chauffeur had finally caught up on an errand he had forgotten the week before. That afternoon the girl chanced to meet Mrs. Mack in the little shopping district of the town.

"Thank you for the roses you sent me," and with emphasis, "I finally got them today."

"Oh, did you like them? I had them in my room for nearly a week, and they were so beautiful and fragrant that I really enjoyed them. Finally they began to wither, and I sent them over to you."

"I don't understand."

"Well, my dear, let me explain. A few nights ago my husband and I were in town on an errand. While he went into the drugstore, I was sitting alone in the car, and I heard some young people walk past. They seemed to be discussing the special meetings we are having this week at church. I heard one of them say that she supposed that one of these years she would give her life to Christ, but that right now, while she was still young, she wanted to enjoy her life."

"I—I could have been the one who said that."

"Yes, and like the roses, you want to enjoy the sweetness and the fragrance of your youth, and then when it is all used up, you plan to give it to Christ."

Powerful stuff.

A third value of illustration is to gain attention. It is as simple as saying, "Let me tell you what happened to me the other day." And for the next fifteen seconds at least you will have the interest and attention of your hearers. As you then launch into your story, you will almost certainly hold that interest. There are many ways to gain attention, and a later chapter will deal with some of them, but a prime way is to tell a story. So much the better if you tell it well, if you know how to develop it, if you build up some suspense, if it involves some element of injustice and if you finish it right. Some of your hearers might be tired and sleepy, but they will probably not drop off during an illustration.

A fourth value of the illustration is to plant an idea that may bring about future action. The chapter on suggestion further along in this book will deal with the whole area in some detail. But to give an example of this use, I once heard a pastor prepare his congregation to discipline a sinning member, and he did it by working into his sermons for several weeks in a row illustrations of churches having to deal with sinning members. As it turned out, the people resolved the specific problem without the church having to make a public issue out of it; but if discipline had been necessary, it appeared that the pastor had prepared the church to carry through with it.

Years ago I saw a revival promoted by just such suggestion. At a certain school a chapel service had lasted nonstop for almost four days. Students from the school I was attending drove out to observe. Next day in our chapel service they gave brief testimonies. Others wanted to speak, and our chapel—with only a supper break—lasted on into the night. It might be argued that some public confessions went beyond New Testament propriety; but most of those who were there believed that revival had taken place, revival touched off by suggestion. Then the following week students gave testimonies of similar revivals taking place over the weekend in their churches, after they or other students had gone home to recount what had happened in our chapel service.

Illustrations can indeed plant ideas.

Sources of Illustrations

In general, you get illustrations from three sources: study, experience and imagination.

A leading source of illustrations is your study life, and your richest source is surely your Bible. We may well wonder if any spiritual experience exists that Scripture does not somewhere reflect. As you study your Bible, you have not only all the Old Testament accounts, but you also have the Lord's own sermon illustrations.

In addition to Bible study, almost any study will suggest illustrations. Almost any reading of history will offer analogies, experiences and examples. Much literature will involve illustrative material—but this also carries some cautions; when a preacher refers to a risqué popular novel (and I have heard this done), he is planting seeds he might not like to harvest. Almost any area of expertise the preacher may ever have studied, from abacus to zoology, can offer useful analogies. Christian and missionary biographies are rich sources.

A second source of illustrations is the preacher's own experience. So long as we are not by our inconsistencies planting wrong impulses, our own experiences can enliven our messages and by our lives accredit our messages. We need to make sure that such illustrations do not feed our own ego ("As I was shaking hands with Prince Philip . . .") or that they do not disclose confidences. A veteran pastor once remarked that his best illustrations were the ones he couldn't use. But within such limitations, our own experiences can be rich sources. Several homiletics students of mine worked nights in hospitals and, without disclosing any confidences, they had no trouble coming in with plenty of fascinating illustrations. But it can be just as easy for those who work on farms or in law enforcement or in almost anything else dealing with the public. The only problem with this might be in too often referring to the years as an army officer or as a mortuary assistant or as a factory worker or whatever.

A third source is imagination. These are the illustrations you dream up and introduce with such words as, "Put yourself in this situation. Suppose you were—" You get these by reflecting hard on the spiritual principle you want to illustrate. Sooner or later your mind will begin to suggest parallel situations. Take the words "How would you feel if—" and build from there.

"Suppose it's night, and you come on the scene of an accident. A car has gone off on the side of the road, and. . . ." Or,

"Put yourself in the place of this widow. You have buried your husband, and all you have left is the house you own. Now this Christian businessman is bringing suit to get it away from you. . . ." Or,

"Let's say that you're the father of the bride, and you have laid out a bundle to put on a really nice wedding for her. . . ."

Take it from there.

The Process of Getting Illustrations

But how do you actually get them? Hardly by leafing through books of them, although it could happen that you find what you are looking for. Rather you work at cultivating an awareness of similarities. Machiavelli mentioned a prince who, on a journey, would halt when sighting a castle or city and discuss with his associates the best military approach to capture it. Similarly, some preachers constantly look for illustrations. One of them was sitting with a group of students from his church as they watched a tiny girl crawl about the rug. He asked, "Now what is the illustration in her? How about this? She may be only a few months old, but she already has all the life that she will ever have. A Christian may be only a few days old in the Lord, but he already has all the regenerate life he will ever have."

Another pastor meticulously files illustrations. He keeps them on cards, arranges them according to topic and notes the date and situation in which he uses them, should he later decide to use one again. For the systematic, this makes an excellent practice. For the hurried, it would probably lead to a guilt trip—and few usable cards.

But however you get them, the moment of need comes as you are completing your sermon skeleton and are looking for means to develop a given point. Stare at it. Wait. Your mind will sooner or later suggest parallel situations. If you do not like what comes up, push it aside and wait for something else. As you pray and then canvas your memory, the illustrations should come.

Qualities of the Illustration

The illustration ought to have a story line. If it does not, it is probably too brief to count as an illustration, even if it does have value as a figure of speech. Count it as an illustration only if it is long enough to build up some interest and generate some suspense. If it doesn't culminate with a sort of tag line, work at it until it does. Be careful of anything that leaves us hanging. Either tie up the loose threads or have a good reason if you choose to wait to tie them up.

Second, we may accept without discussion or proof that an illustration should clearly and obviously bear out the idea that it illustrates. We can all think of examples of this matter, many of them unfortunate.

Third, while an illustration does not need to be true—an imagined event need not have happened—it should be honest and humble. Honest, in that no one should be able to call the preacher a liar upon hearing it, and honest in that if it draws upon actual events, it does not distort the truth, particularly in the preacher's favor. Since illustrations can be ego trips, it is Scriptural to shade them on the side of modesty. In 2 Corinthians 12:2 Paul said, "I knew a man in Christ. . . ." That statement suggests that a preacher is doing no damage to the truth if instead of putting himself in too brilliant a light, he begins his story with the words, "Let me tell you what happened to a man I know." When we hear just so much about a preacher's repartee, his degrees, his travels abroad, his marksmanship, his clever financial dealings, even the revivals he has caused, we tend to have trouble sharing his admiration for himself.

Fourth, the illustration ought to be plausible, and some are not. Certain remarks attributed to children strain our credulity. Certain coincidences, certain vagaries of the human soul, are hard to believe. If you think that an illustration falls into this class, you have two choices: either leave it out or else introduce it in words that prepare us for the unusual. "Now listen, I know that this might happen only once in a hundred years, but. . . ." Or "Now stay with me. My father-in-law was present when the police got there, and this is what really happened." If you simply tell about the woman who jumped an eight-foot fence, a fair number of your hearers will turn you off. If you point out that the factory hands on lunch break witnessed the argument, saw the husband with the bread knife and measured the fence, you probably retain everyone's confidence, not to say a measure of interest.

Fifth, the illustration should be in good taste. This, too, goes without needing discussion or proof. The Lord could be extremely severe, but He was never in bad taste. Since situations differ, what might be appropriate to a weekend youth retreat might not sound right in a Sunday morning service.

Sixth, and this one is particularly important, an illustration should ideally be a concrete example of spiritual experience. Some illustrations are analogies of spiritual experience, such as all of the seven parables in Matthew 13 or the parable of the wicked husbandmen in Matthew 21. Other parables are personal examples, such as the account of the good Samaritan, the Prodigal Son and his brother or the rich man and Lazarus (which does not qualify as a parable). Since the Lord used analogies, they surely must be defensible. But some reflection ought to bear out the observation that personal experiences have greater impact. If you tell about how a little dirt in a carburetor filter can stop your car—some of us have had it happen—you can show the effect of a little unconfessed sin on a Christian's life. On the other hand, if you tell about the missionary who found himself helpless when a villager called him to rebuke the powers of darkness and how his ministry was restored only after he apologized to a fellow missionary, you are dealing with something closer to the heart. The concrete example enables us to identify with a fellow-mortal who went through something we have been through or could go through. It also has the advantage of helping us feel that we are less alone in our walk with God, that other people have trials like ours and that their victories help us believe that victories are possible for us too.

What about the illustration that is too good? It totally grips attention and imagination. Perhaps it deals with an injustice. The story about Mrs. Mack and the flowers is probably an example of this. When you have finished and gone on to something else, your hearers are still thinking about your story. You probably won't be aware of the problem, but awareness is most of the solution. Do anything. Snap your fingers. Ask them to follow you, but somehow get their attention back.

And one other caution applies to the illustration that we are tempted to use that deals with persons known to our congregation. This is a temptation we dare not yield to, if for no other reason than the damage it can do to people, not to mention the damage it can do to ourselves. If it puts our member in a good light, it might be justifiable. All too often, however, the thinly disguised example drawn from our counseling can disclose confidences that will never be forgiven. In this way men have soiled their ministries and lost members. We may be glad that not many make this mistake, but those who do seem never to learn.

QUESTIONS FOR DISCUSSION

1. Which preachers have you known whose illustrations particularly impressed you? How did they do it?

2. Why do analogies of spiritual experience seem easier to find than concrete examples? Are the concrete examples really better? Then how do we get them?

3. What advice can you give to the preacher who insists that he simply can't think up or remember illustrations?

4. If while preparing a sermon you do not get much help from a book of illustrations, can you in any way get value out of it?

5. In what ways can good illustrations add holy passion to a sermon?

CHAPTER 8

ON GETTING INTEREST

You're going to preach tonight in your regular evening service. Of the men who come, all but a handful have spent the afternoon watching professional football. They arrive at church with their minds full of extraneous images: plays, game strategies, girls, commercials, violence—all in color. The evening service moves through songs, testimonies, offering and special music. Now how can you preach so as to get past the gaudy forms that crowd their minds?

It's your move.

We are not called to be showmen, and we had better fight the impulse to regard preaching as a performing art. The Bible does deal with the acting profession, but the New Testament word for actor is worth more study than it seems to be getting. When the Devil invited Jesus to put on a spectacular and jump from the temple cornice, He rebuked him and refused to do it. For all the miracles Jesus worked, when Herod wanted to watch one, the Lord stood silent. When the crowds asked a sign from Heaven, He answered that an evil and adulterous generation seeks a sign. On the one hand, if we do not grip attention and interest, we might as well not preach. But on the other hand, if we preach in the flesh and rely on carnal means to get attention, we concede the field to the Enemy.

Somehow we must steer between both dangers. We cannot afford to be dull, but neither can we permit ourselves to become entertainers. People may come to hear us on that basis, as Ezekiel found, but that is their responsibility before God, and we must not feed their impulse, much as we may be tempted to. God said to Ezekiel,

> And they come unto thee as the people cometh, and they sit before thee as my people, and they hear thy words, but they will not do them: for with their mouth they shew much love, but their heart goeth after their covetousness. And, lo, thou art unto them as a very lovely song of one that hath a pleasant voice, and can play well on an instrument: for they hear thy words, but they do them not. And when this cometh to pass, (lo, it will come,) then shall they know that a prophet hath been among them (Ezek. 33:31–33).

On Getting Interest

For at least twenty-five centuries some of God's people have supposed that His work is a form of entertainment. Whatever our temptation, we yield to it at spiritual peril. Since discernment seems to be in short supply, let us pray for discernment, especially at this point.

We may suppose three levels of attention. The attention we might make ourselves give to a lecturer or to a textbook is voluntary. The attention we give to a novel or to a demonstration may be involuntary. The attention we give to a hobby rises to interest. New Christians often testify to their fascination with Bible study so that what to many people requires voluntary attention, to new Christians may become interest.

Much current preaching requires voluntary attention. Some might make a case for that voluntary attention on the grounds that it should tend to toughen the sheep and drive off the goats. Those saints who make themselves listen to tedious discourse must surely live on a higher spiritual plane as a result of their holy resolve, and thus flat preaching invites people to rise above the level of the carnal hearers around them. Those who yawn and do not come back must be written off as being in the flesh, people the church is better off without. Perhaps. But blessed are the merciful, for they shall obtain mercy; and that text probably applies here. When Eutychus went to sleep, it was not because Paul was a tedious preacher. Some preachers rise to the level of Paul and the prophets and hold attention. One might get the impression that before World War II such preaching happened more often than now.

Some sermons have such a grip that they transcend attention; they draw interest. Mainly these deal with sensitive subjects, such as Jonathan Edwards's sermon to the church that had just voted him out. I doubt that anyone present missed a word of it. Another example is the situation in which a black preacher addresses a white audience on the implications of racial intermarriage. The tension gets high, the attention rapt.

By what means then can we get and hold the attention and interest of our hearers?

How Can You Get Your Audience's Attention?

Spiritual Urgency

"How shall they hear without a preacher?" If we really believe that our preaching is the most important thing we do, this conviction will show itself in our very presence. By dozens of cues, unknown to us, our voice and our body language will carry this message of honest urgency; and this message is compelling. It overrides fear. It covers awkward gestures and mistakes in grammar. Without this conviction our preaching will have all the fizz of the ginger ale someone uncapped last week. With this conviction we will usually carry our people with us. Whether we preach fast or slow, whether we are loud or soft, we will have a certain intensity that gets across.

How do we get the conviction? The whole intent of this book is to answer that question, beginning with our confidence that God has called us. If you are preaching, it is probably because you have somehow come to the conviction that God has individually called you to do it, whatever else He might lead you to do. But you start with this. That is what chapter 1 was all about.

On this conviction you base a second one—the conviction that in this occasion you have a message from God, a message that these people need. As you found in chapter 2, when you have spent time with God, and when you have mastered the passage at hand, a certainty should grip you. And this certainty is the basis on which you will hold your hearers. No use working it up, and little use preaching without it. Without this urgency, can we even call it preaching?

What about when Paul spoke of his ministry in Corinth as being in weakness, fear and much trembling? A careful reading of 1 Corinthians 2:1–3 shows that Paul himself was indeed with them in weakness, fear and trembling. As to his preaching, the next verse says, "And my speech and my preaching was not with enticing words of man's wisdom, but in demonstration of the Spirit and of power: that your faith should not stand in the wisdom of men, but in the power of God" (vv. 4, 5). In 2 Corinthians 7:4 he said, "Great is my boldness of speech toward you." In 1 Thessalonians 2:2 and 3, he stated, "But even after that we had suffered before, and were shamefully entreated, as ye know, at Philippi, we were bold in our God to speak unto you the gospel of God with much contention. For our exhortation was not of deceit, nor of uncleanness, nor in guile."

Close to these matters is another that deserves more class discussion than it seems to get: Is it spiritually important? While chapter 5 touched on the question, it is a vital concern again at the point of holding interest. What makes a matter spiritually important? In one sense every truth in Scripture is important and needs only reflection for the preacher to see it and bring out its urgency. In the wrong hands almost any truth can be made to plod along, and in other hands the same truth will vibrate with urgency.

In another sense, however, the discerning preacher will note those truths that have gone unnoticed, and he will preach them with freshness. This ability accounts for the popularity of several esteemed conference speakers. George MacDonald wrote that Jesus never thought of being original. That may be true, but it probably never occurred to those who heard Him speak. All He said came across as spiritually important, and the crowds listened.

Expertise

A second legitimate element in holding attention is a unique grasp of the subject at hand. Get an expert, and while he is talking in his field, he has to be unusually dull not to hold attention. Consult your memory and see if you cannot remember numbers of times when speakers held your attention simply by their detailed knowledge of their subject. In my own experience, the ones who come to mind are a specialist on civil defense, a mathematician, a rabbi (comparing Jewish theology with Christian), two medical doctors, two psychologists, an attorney, several journalists and various teachers.

What these people had in common was that they thoroughly knew their subjects, either by a lifetime of study or by careful homework. I suppose that the keys in these situations are a command of detail, a few brilliant generalizations and a wealth of personal experiences. What negates the expertise are too many generalizations, material that is too abstract or professional jargon and talking down to the audience.

How does this carry into our preaching? Chiefly at two points: by our lifetime acquaintance with God and by our faithful homework every time we expound His Word.

Communication

The word "communicate" has become a jargon word in the same class with parameter, finalize and nitty-gritty, but it can still denote an ability that some speakers have and that all need to have. To speak of someone as a communicator says that he knows how to speak directly to a group and get his ideas across. This book treats the matter in a later chapter, but mention belongs here.

A communicator speaks directly. He keeps eye contact. Even at full volume, his speech patterns follow those of conversation, not proclamation. He talks to his hearers; he does not merely intone words in their presence. It is easy to listen to a communicator, partly because he uses many means to hold his hearers, but largely because his actual manner of getting his ideas into our minds makes it easy for us to listen.

A communicator involves his hearers. He talks to us in terms of our needs, our experiences, our feelings, our desires. At the carnal level, this answers to the dictum, "Talk to a man about himself, and he will sit and listen for hours." On a more spiritual level, read Paul's address to the Ephesian elders (Acts 20) and note how he involved them. His first word is "Ye," and in the King James Version he goes on to mention them another eighteen times.

A major part of communication is just that—talking to people in terms of their interests. You often find yourself using such expressions as

"Put yourself in Timothy's place."

"How do you feel when someone says to you—?"

"Have you ever been in a situation where you wanted to get through to God, but you felt utterly alone?"

"What does it do to you when—?"

"Now that you have read the book of Romans, you understand something of this principle."

"When was the last time you went through something like this?"

Decision

A previous chapter dealt with preaching for decision. Whatever other values such preaching may have, it tends to keep people awake. Even if they did not like all they heard, and even if they give you a cold handshake at the door, it means that they didn't go to sleep while you pressed God's claims on them.

Asking for Attention

One way to get attention, for the moment at least, is simply to ask for it. About 250 times in the Old Testament the writers or speakers said such things as "Hearken unto me" or "Hear, O Israel!" You find similar expressions from Jesus, Peter, Stephen, Paul and James. When you point up an important statement with, "Now listen to this," you have about fifteen seconds of attention by this means alone.

Humor

One of your surest devices for holding attention is humor, but it can also be spiritually dangerous. A man who has just come from the Holy Place doesn't have much to joke about. The Bible is a serious book, and such traces of humor as it contains are not easy to find. The preacher who begins his sermon with five jokes in rapid fire is on his own; he would have a tough time finding Scripture to justify his approach.

With that caution, the alert mind will forever be seeing the incongruities in life, and a merry heart doeth good like a medicine. The servant of God must rest on Him for wisdom to know how much humor is enough. Humor helps to hold interest, and in the form of irony it is a powerful figure of speech. Humor makes our hearers feel good and feel good toward us.

This last touches the temptation to the flesh. The response of the audience can have an alcoholic effect on a speaker, and the popular song declaring that there is no business like show business is probably right. Some men and women have a natural ability to sway a crowd, an ability that can draw far more from a grasp of human nature than from reliance on the Holy Spirit. If an audience responds to our humor, let us guard our caution and remind ourselves that the message of the Cross is not a form of entertainment.

Material Inherently Interesting

What applies to humor applies to certain other kinds of material that of their own nature grip our interest. Examples of these appear in the Bible. However, as we actually use this sort of material, let us trust for the discernment to know if we are getting it in response to believing prayer or not.

Narrative is interesting. Just say, "Let me tell you what happened to me the other day," and you have us. You tell a story, and if you tell it even moderately well, you hold us. It is up to you to determine how well it fits your sermonic purpose; but a story line at least helps us stay awake. Every real illustration has a story line, and this enables it to hold our interest, a function in addition to those of clarifying or amplifying a point. And narrative is evidently Scriptural; the Bible is full of it.

Another kind of material inherently interesting is almost anything that has to do with animals. This seems to be true for two reasons. For one, we constantly see in animal behavior reflections of our own. For another, animal behavior is mysterious. As I write this, robins are maintaining a nest not eight feet from my window and warming four eggs. We are daily confronted with the mystery of their ways. Why do they build? Why does the male robin share the work? And then, why does a dog's affection differ from a cat's? How much do animals remember? When the Bible, especially the Old Testament, gives quite a bit of material about animals, we help our people stay awake by using animal stories to illustrate Scriptural truth.

For similar reasons, the uncanny is interesting material. While the Bible warns us about interesting ourselves in the occult, it does speak of the mysteries of life and death. To the uninitiated, the mysteries of mathematics and electronics are as fascinating as stories about the powers of darkness and are far safer for our people's minds.

The themes of love and hate can grip interest. If the treatment is awkward, we lose. If we can show love as an intention, we gain. Our generation has so much confused love with the erotic that hardly anyone seems to know what love is. Stories that deal with love share some of the mystery of the animals and the uncanny. Why does a person spend himself to purpose the happiness of the one he loves?

The college was giving the seniors a long, comprehensive exam. A proctor noticed a student pulling out his wallet and consulting something. The student did it again. The proctor carefully worked his way behind the suspect. Again the student drew out his wallet—to look at the picture of the girl whose future, with his own, turned on his success with this examination. O. Henry's story "The Gift of the Magi" is better yet.

On the other hand, such themes as hate, cruelty and injustice may be unpleasant to deal with, but the Bible treats these sins. They occur naturally in the human heart, and they draw interest. No wonder that Nathan's story about the poor man's lamb got David's attention or Joab's story from the lips of the wise woman. For maximum impact you need to build it up with detail and then take such a seemingly neutral stand that your hearers supply their own moral indignation. Your next problem will be to regain the attention you focused on your story. For this reason these illustrations can be too good; they continue to fascinate your people when you have already moved to another matter.

Prediction is another kind of material that gets interest. Of all the reasons to preach prophecy, the strongest is that the Bible contains it, and we have the command to preach the Bible. But most people seem genuinely concerned about what is ahead. A missionary to Europe told me that prophecy is his most useful topic when it comes to building attendance in a home Bible study.

How many predictions of our own may we hazard? The best caution seems to be to draw inferences with care. Mussolini did not turn out to be the Antichrist. On the other hand, a century ago George N. H. Peters in his *The Theocratic Kingdom* drew some shrewd inferences and predicted about thirty-eight trends to come before the second coming of Christ. His surprising accuracy is evidence that careful scholarship can make useful predictions about the future. Because predictions share with other kinds of material the element of mystery, they do help to hold the attention and interest of our people.

Suspense

In holding an audience, some preachers are good at creating suspense. Suspense means promising something and then deferring payment. "How long will you keep us in suspense? If you are the Christ, tell us plainly" (John 10:24, NIV). First, suspense arouses a curiosity, raises a doubt, creates a problem. "Have you ever been involved in digging up a body?" Or, "My friend's daughter was the absolute picture of innocent girlhood, and then she met that fellow." Or, "Would you care to learn how to steal a church?"

Next, you take time to build the suspense. A man I once taught with was a master at this. He would arouse a class's curiosity about a spiritual problem. Then he would bring up possible solutions, and after building each one, he would demolish it. All the while he would tease the class by asking, "Would you like to know the answer? Would you? Well, have you considered this possibility?" His final solutions were as unforgettable as his method.

Third, suspense requires the careful selection of details. This is true especially in narration. If you try to build with easy generalities, you face a tough task. On the other hand, I have listened repeatedly to a tape of Robert G. Lee's famous sermon, "Payday Someday." Much of its fascination lies in its use of details, imaginatively but legitimately drawn from the Biblical account of Ahab's itch to get Naboth's vineyard and Jezebel's helpfulness. Suspense indeed. It can be done.

The Polarized Audience

The ultimate level of attention will be discussed in the later chapter on suggestion: that of the polarized audience. Packed close, admiring the speaker, intent on his words, the members respond together. If you have watched it happen, you know it is powerful stuff. The audience becomes highly suggestible. If while you preach you realize that the audience is polarizing, guard your humility and trust God for responses. Both prophets and charlatans have moved their audiences this way before you.

How Do You Preach Bible Exposition to People Who Are Not Used to Bible Exposition?

Not so long ago a man was discussing with a fellow teacher the regrettable decline in the Bible conference movement. At mid-century we had in the United States something like 150 major Bible conferences, most of them premillennial, and most of them thriving. The teacher's explanation has to be on target: If people are not cultivating a taste for Bible exposition in their own churches, why should they drive across the state to hear it?

So you are the pulpit supply or the pulpit candidate or the new preacher. If it is a strange church altogether, you can probably go on the working basis that the people are unprepared for an expository ministry. Eventually a child gets to eat beef, potatoes and vegetables; but this is not the food for a newborn. Paul wrote in this vein to the church at Corinth. What to do? One possibility is to sell out and give them what they are probably open to, meaning a commentary on a verse, peppered with illustrations and salted with humor. Flattery might work, but Paul rules that out in 1 Thessalonians 2. We preach under the command of 2 Timothy 4:2, "Preach the word."

A possible solution, with the sanction of the Lord's own example, comes in Mark 4:33 and 34: "And with many such parables spake he the word unto them, as they were able to hear it. But without a parable spake he not unto them: and when they were alone, he expounded all things to his disciples."

This suggestive remark implied several principles.

1. Some people are simply not ready for spiritual truth. To paraphrase

the end of verse 33, "Just as they had the power to go on hearing." There is an ability that some do not have. They might have the ability to hear for a few moments; they do not have the ability to follow an extended discourse. The Lord did not expect them to take extended discourse.

2. We preach and teach at various levels of content. What would have choked the crowds was what fed the disciples.

3. To the crowds Jesus preached in parables. Those who were interested could apparently stay for the explanation He gave afterward to the smaller circle.

4. To those who cannot yet follow Bible exposition, we do well also to preach with illustrations.

What we do well to avoid is the practice of a popular preacher of the last generation. He preached illustrations, indeed, but their point seemed far less to clarify Scripture than to warm his own ego. Three long stories about himself and a gospel invitation made the evening.

If the Lord's parables had been chiefly to glorify Himself, we could rejoice in that case that they served a Scriptural principle—bringing honor to the Lamb. Rather His parables seem chiefly to clarify Biblical truth and to make it vivid. What all this suggests to us is the value of preparing expository outlines but developing them with extended illustrations. For the introduction, try the mental feat of remembering or constructing a story that attracts interest and that pictures the truth in the opening verses of your passage. This leads to your proposition, your transition and your first main head. You announce the head, perhaps repeat it and read the verses you drew it from, and now you launch into another story. This one, too, is crafted to draw interest and to illustrate the principle in those verses. So on through your message. This discipline will stretch your mind to come up with just the right illustrations, and they are one way to introduce your people to Bible exposition. During the months to follow, you can discreetly reduce the illustrations and increase the explanations.

If someone should ask where you get all those extended illustrations, each one explaining or picturing whole verses, the answer might well be, "Who said sermon preparation was easy? Shall we offer unto the Lord that which cost us nothing?" It will take real work to exegete the passage. It will take even more work to find or to invent the stories that will explain the passage. If we can remember persons we know who have experienced the truth at hand, so much the better. Those experiences can provide the insights that make people understand.

While that will take work, it should pay off in giving people a fresh taste for Bible exposition. In the process as it increases our confidence in the message itself, it may also pay off in added passion to convey the truth to those who need it.

QUESTIONS FOR DISCUSSION

1. What preachers can you think of, past or present, who have been good at gripping attention? How did they do it?

2. In building up Bible stories with imaginative detail, what guidelines should govern us?

3. What other means can you think of for getting attention? How well do the striking statement or the probing question work?

4. How would you set about to get the interest of a group of teenagers?

5. For the whole intent of this chapter, what cautions do you see?

CHAPTER 9

WHAT DOES DELIVERY HAVE TO DO WITH IT?

A chapter in a book is a pale substitute for a course in public speaking. On the other hand, it is possible to take the course and still need the chapter. Some things presented in class may not "take," and problems can arise later, the preacher all unawares. These problems can be extremely damaging when the preacher is most sensitive about anyone calling them to his attention. After all, parents are sensitive about their children, writers about their articles and surgeons about their surgeries. However, while parents learn to discipline, while writers revise their work and while surgeons do autopsies, we may wonder how many preachers critique their own preaching.

Our own postmortems are not inordinately expensive. Surely you own a cassette recorder, and it can reveal a great deal. How many churches already have recorders in their sound systems? Better yet, you can rent a portable video camera for the weekend from your friendly local dealer if you don't have one already. Set it up in the back of your auditorium—it doesn't have to be all that noticeable—and you can find out in living color what your people see and hear. (Incidentally, you might seriously consider a video ministry for shut-ins if your church doesn't already offer it.)

To diagnose and improve your delivery, the cassette recorder will tell you some of the story; the video will, of course, tell you a lot more. But one thing we all know: It is especially difficult to concentrate on preaching a sermon and at the same time on correcting and improving delivery. The rest of this chapter will make a lot more sense, therefore, if you have the use of the gadgetry.

A second thing we all know is that the power of an honestly burdened heart can transcend many delivery problems. Whitefield was cross-eyed. Uncle Bud Robinson lisped. You can think of your own examples of men of God whose preaching blessed you so much that you hardly noticed the reedy voice, the odd gestures or the nervous tics.

With that said, certain common problems are worth considering, and if you have any of them, almost all are subject to treatment. Let's begin with the voice.

Pitch

Of the problems with voice, too-high pitch is probably the most common—and perhaps the most damaging. When the preacher's voice moves from the baritone into the tenor range, he begins to lose authority and to convey weakness. Surprisingly few speakers know how to increase volume without raising pitch. While a few peaks in the tenor range are not serious, letting the average or overall pitch go up has several dangers. Besides conveying weakness, it also strains, tires and possibly even damages the vocal bands. More than one preacher has talked by phone with strangers and wondered why some of them addressed him as "Ma'am." What's more, the high pitch tends to annoy some people, who probably could not give a specific reason for their lack of respect for the speaker. Another problem for the man who preaches in the upper tenor range is that if he should want to stress something, he has nowhere else to go.

So how do you deal with pitch? The working rule is that your best average pitch is the lowest you can use without strain. To reach this, think baritone, not tenor. Work at speaking in the baritone range. Practice in private, reading and speaking in baritone range, breathing from the belt and sometimes pouring on the volume. Have your recorder on so that you can hear yourself. Read a chapter, raising and lowering your pitch to get a new feel of how your voice works. Then practice volume, keeping pitch down; try it louder and softer.

In both 1980 and 1984 Ronald Reagan performed superbly on the platforms and before the cameras, especially in keeping his pitch down. By comparison, both his opponents sounded weak and uncertain. Either of them might have gained a million votes for each note he lowered his pitch.

Loudness

The accepted rule for volume is to speak loudly enough that the people present can hear you.

If you do not speak loudly enough, someone will probably tell you after the service. By then it will be too late. Those who cannot hear the message will find the situation deeply annoying. The preacher who is barely loud enough and then drops his voice at the end of sentences is almost as annoying.

If you speak too loudly, people might not be so quick to tell you. Few people like to be yelled at; only the hard-of-hearing will be grateful. To the rest you will be an annoyance, and some of them will go out with headaches from the noise. Real headaches. Some of them will not be back.

Problems with volume are difficult to treat—surprisingly difficult—because a man's habitual volume level is so comfortable to him that he can hardly believe that others do not share his comfort. If he is not loud enough, he probably feels that any more volume would drive his hearers against the walls. If he is too loud, he probably feels that any less volume would not get his ideas across. These three suggestions would seem to be more self-evident than they are:

1. If your auditorium has a sound system, make sure that it can be controlled from some other place than the platform. Your sound man can then compensate for any problems. An amplifier in the pulpit is in the worst possible place; nobody who might be able to set it at the right volume can get near it. The additional problem is the heat that rises from it all through the services.

2. Lacking that, you can arrange with a friendly usher to signal you from the back when the volume is wrong.

3. Never speak as loudly as you could; always hold something in reserve. This applies also to pitch. When you use all your force you lose authority, even if the point seemed so important as to deserve all that stress. This may seem to contradict the principle of total commitment to Christian service and putting all we have into our preaching.

There is no contradiction here. Total commitment to Christ means serving with pure motives, with no private games we are playing on the side. Control of loudness has to do with temperance or self-discipline, which is part of the fruit of the Spirit (Gal. 5:23). To yell from the pulpit as loudly as we can is not only a breach of temperance, it is almost in the same class as getting angry or belittling our people. Any of these will cost us respect.

Quality

Of all the descriptive words that apply to voice quality, probably

Delivery

"hoarse" describes the hardest problem to deal with. Hoarseness comes from a rough surface on the vocal bands. If you just need to clear your throat, simple. If hoarseness comes from infection or shouting, it needs healing. If it comes from a lifetime of abuse, you live with it.

Qualities of timbre, resonance and nasality can yield to control. As you listen to your recorded voice, what do you hear? Once a men's quartet was practicing. At one point the bass asked the leader about his tone, "Do you want me to put a hard glaze on it?"

If you detect that your tone is ministerial and breathy ("holy tones"), how do you deal with that? Probably the best answer is to come back to reality; work at teaching your people, not at trying to impress them. The same applies if you realize that on tape you sound like an auctioneer or a barker. Auctioneers need skill and practice to perform, but your own experience should tell you that they use their chants only for calling bids, not for conversation or for conveying the riches of divine truth.

Pronunciation

In this culture that has denied all absolutes, even the rebels of society do not like to hear words mispronounced. It should take no great discernment to identify the leaders in any community, the ones who set the standards of taste and usage. To disregard those standards is to limit our ministries.

A missionary told how his field leader looked to the provinces for the "real" language of the country. For the mission broadcast over the capital radio station, the leader chose a Bible school student from a remote village to do the preaching. To be sure, the student preached with verve and authority and in the authentic language of the people who lived in the boondocks. One day the missionary happened to be on a minibus riding through the capital, and the bus radio was tuned to the mission program. The sermon had hardly begun when at some expression all the passengers clapped their hands over their ears. The driver tuned to a different station. The mission learned the hard way.

So who sets the standards? Mainly the community leaders of the middle and upper middle class, the ones who tend to become the core of solid churches. The poor heard Jesus gladly, but they are not the ones who set the standards of pronunciation. If you pronounce words according to the standards of the community, you will still reach the poor, but you will not try the patience of those who have proved to be your most stable backers. If you preach that people need to "get borned again," do not think that you are helping your message—even if some respond to the invitation. Sincerity will transcend a multitude of mispronunciations (witness the power of D. L. Moody), but not many preachers using poor English are D. L. Moodys. In the meantime, listen for the language of the serious, and trust your dictionary.

Enunciation

There may be such a thing as enunciating too distinctly, trying so hard to speak distinctly as to lose the easy flow of a communicator's delivery. Speech may sound overly studied and contrived, and this goes with lack of passion.

The more common problem, however, is careless enunciation, mumbling words and running words together. If you detect this as you listen to your sermons, you may feel comfortable with the habit you have, but you may also feel like a man in tuxedo and tennis shoes. In this case, you simply force yourself to work at enunciating, and you save the contractions for the rare case when emphasis might call for one or for when you are quoting someone else.

Rate

Problems in rate come down to about three: too fast, too slow or jerky.

If you think you may be preaching too fast, in pulpit passion it is no surprise if the words come in torrents. As you listen to the cassette, you might well ask, Is the enunciation clear enough for the speed? How many ideas am I repeating? Is this too fast for the people to hear and understand? If the gush of words passes these tests, thank God for the passion and keep preaching. Otherwise, slow down.

What if your preaching is too slow? If you think slowly, you may not be able to do much about preaching slowly. That said, it would seem that too-slow preaching comes down to three problems: (1) lack of preparation, leading to a lack of content and the need to stretch ten minutes' worth of content to make a thirty-minute sermon. (2) Lack of prayer, causing a lack of passion. This may have something to do with the common inability to get excited about divine truth. It may also have something to do with certain long pulpit prayers, as the pastor has the personal devotions he did not have in his closet. (3) A third possible cause

Delivery

of slow preaching is the careful, self-conscious delivery of a man deeply concerned about how he looks. He is so careful not to make a verbal mistake that he seems to contrive every word and gesture. All three of those can be treated but at real cost in spiritual effort.

A third problem, a jerky delivery, seems more likely to occur in the young preacher. His ideas come in bursts and so does his sermon. If you detect this in your preaching, just being aware of it is about half the battle; just think toward a smooth flow. When you need to pause, pause, as when you have just asked a rhetorical question. Give us time to think of an answer. The new preacher keeps preaching to fill the silence. The experienced preacher has confidence and poise for the situation.

What if you articulate your pauses? In conversation it seems to be a necessary way to hold the floor while you frame what to say next. From the platform it tends to annoy your hearers. The best defenses are (1) to try to break the "uh" or "OK" habit; and (2) to try to frame your thoughts further in advance. Writing tends to give choice of words, but beware of reading sermons from the pulpit.

Stance

Stand tall. If you lean forward, do it for emphasis and not because you slump. If, like John Knox, you are deathly sick and need two young men to carry you into the pulpit, your people will excuse you for leaning on it. If you preach with Knox's passion, you will not be leaning on it for more than the first few minutes.

If you find yourself leaning back from the pulpit, ask yourself why you feel on the defensive.

Gestures

Probably the best rule for gestures is that they should look easy and natural, not forced and contrived. This means that your message calls them forth; you gesture as you have to. If you watch the video tape and the gestures do not look right, or if they are at the level of your pants' pockets, take the time right then to give them thought and to improve them.

Motion

How much should you move around the platform? If you are a nervous person, you will probably want to stay in motion. Probably the two leading considerations are (1) that you come to terms with the sound system and stay near the microphone; (2) if the video shows that your motion seems aimless, use your move to emphasize something and don't just wander around the platform or rock back and forth. Moving or striding becomes a sort of gesture, and you do it with purpose.

On the other hand, if the video makes you look like something carved from oak, figure out a way to relax, to loosen up and to move when you need to stress something.

Eye Contact

The words of the renowned Dr. Charles Koller to his senior preaching class ring in his students' ears: "Preach to the whites of their eyes." Sound advice.

Eye contact is important in so many ways that we need to begrudge every instant that we look away from the faces of our people. It projects our own concern for them. It helps hold their attention and gives us some measure of control over the whisperers in the back rows. It conveys confidence and authority. It gives us a chance to follow what is going on in the building, at least if we are not concentrating too much on the sermon to understand. Ideally we should be able to get feedback from our hearers, and while eye contact does not guarantee our picking up that feedback, a lack of eye contact will guarantee that we will not get any feedback.

Despite all this some preachers only occasionally look at their congregations. A well-known pastor and conference speaker used to preach to two imaginary galleries, one to his right and the other to his left. In a moment of candor someone asked him why he did not work on eye contact. He answered that an old teacher of his had advised him never to look at his people, that he would forget the train of his message. Can anyone imagine worse advice to give to a young preacher?

Time was when a preacher was expected to write his sermons out in full and read them. Apparently the custom began during the persecution of the Puritans. A preacher could be hauled into court on Monday for what he was heard to say the day before. To stay out of jail might depend on his ability to show in writing what he had actually preached. Now, however, we have little justification for so reading. This habit permits a preacher to look away from his manuscript barely half the time, and when he does look up, he might not notice the glazed boredom all over his congregation. Whatever the values of writing out one's sermons, the lack of eye contact destroys much of those values. What is worse, the message may sound as if it had already been read to the preacher's former church or churches.

How do you cultivate eye contact with your people? It begins in your study, as you get a fresh burden and as you prepare completely. Another chapter deals with preaching without notes. But even if you carry your notes into the pulpit, careful preparation will enable you to preach without more than the barest glance at them. As you intercede for your congregation, ask God for a fresh love for them. A genuine concern for their need of your message should help you preach directly to them.

Then as you begin to preach, resolve to keep your eyes on them. If it helps to single out several friendly faces around the group and look especially at them, so much the better. If you consult your watch, have it up on the pulpit above your Bible so as to divert your eyes as little as possible. Again, begrudge every instant you take your eyes off your people. Preach to the whites of their eyes.

Manner

An old, apocryphal story had it that a pulpit supply once preached on Hell, from Revelation 20:15. After the sermon a deacon went to him and said, quivering with emotion, "I hope you never preach in our church again!" The following week another pulpit supply announced his text as Revelation 20:15, and he, too, preached on Hell. During the sermon numbers of the members sat in suspense, wondering what sort of confrontation would follow that service. After the invitation the deacon tearfully thanked the preacher for his wonderful message from the Word. A bystander asked the deacon, "How can you say that? Last week you stormed at the man we had, and he preached on the same thing."

"True, but this man today preached as though he cared."

A lot depends on your manner. If you care about your people and about their grasp of your sermon, however earnest you feel, you will convey warmth. On the other hand, if you feel clinical, detached or peeved, this will probably come across. You will not have to try to be strident, harsh or cold, but some of these qualities will convey themselves. If we can choose warmth or chill, Scripture would seem to be on the side of warmth. Whatever we may make of the manner of John the Baptist, when Jesus preached at Nazareth, the people marveled at the words of grace that came from His mouth (Luke 4:22). When Stephen before the Sanhedrin had the face of an angel, we can hardly suppose that he looked like the death angel (Acts 6:15). Jeremiah and Paul preached with tears. If as you watch the video of your sermon you see that you didn't smile much, you might still have been warm. If you were scowling a great deal, you probably need to pray for a new love for your people and for a new passion, a warm passion, for the messages you preach.

As you consider your manner, you might ask again how much of self is shining through. If the preacher is on an ego trip, this will show itself, though probably not to him. Anything that massages the ego will probably seem so comfortable that it will also seem normal and pardonable. Well, should you talk about yourself at all? Should you ask pardon for the personal reference? Paul used his own experiences, and so should you, to the extent that your experiences accredit you to preach the claims of Christ. Let us recognize our limitless ability to justify ourselves, our constant bent to shade the truth in our own favor; and then let us trust God for the discernment to know when to talk about ourselves and when not to. If we can keep pointing men to Christ and keep concerning ourselves for their welfare, we can hope to guard our sense of humor in regard to ourselves.

At the close of this chapter, two principles would stand out. First, we ought for various reasons to try to improve our preaching. This includes eliminating those things that may distract our hearers and turn them off from the truth we preach. This is a constant process, because as we conquer some problems, we tend to pick up others unawares. We pick up new pet phrases to repeat. We pick up habitual gestures and facial expressions, comfortable to us but annoying to others.

A second principle that comforts us is that love covers a multitude of quirks. We can all think of men we know whose people could overlook and forgive problems in delivery because love reigned in their ministries. We can also remember the reverse—men who were asked to leave. Their speech faults were not so great, but their love was not enough to cover those faults. If we genuinely concern ourselves for our people, if we really meet God over our preaching, we can rightly hope that they will forgive our mannerisms and still obey the Word we preach.

QUESTIONS FOR DISCUSSION

1. Why does the Bible say so little about the prophets' delivery?

2. If we have the power of the Holy Spirit, do we need to pay attention to delivery?

3. How much can a person do to improve the timbre of his voice? To what extent can he deal with a nasal problem?

4. How can you improve the mechanics of your delivery without becoming mechanical in your delivery?

5. Comment on this statement: "After all the years he has been in the ministry, if he can't do any better than this he will never improve."

CHAPTER 10

ON BEING A COMMUNICATOR

You're listening to a dear friend preach. You want him to score; you are yearning after him to do a good job. Then you look around to sense what is happening around you. Practically nothing. People do not seem to be following his sermon. Some sit with glazed eyes. Nobody is taking notes, and some have closed their Bibles. He is simply not communicating, and you sit and grieve for him.

So how do we get the eternal claims across? How can a person be a communicator?

By about the year A.D. 400, the liturgical churches arrived at a sort of solution. They standardized the ritual of the mass so that anywhere in the world that a person might go to church, he heard what every other churchgoer heard. He heard some of the service chanted. Why chanted? Because they had no public address system, and the words in the chant seemed to carry farther and without the losses that took place when the preacher lowered his voice. But to us the chant is no solution, even if we can think of preaching that sounded like chanting. It surely has no fire.

How do we communicate, especially in a familiar and structured situation? It is one thing to preach through jail bars or in the open air; it's something else to preach in a church building, at a scheduled time, for so many minutes, on a platform with a pulpit, according to a printed bulletin and the custom of years. I once talked with a pastor who has fifth-generation members in his church; and what a body of traditions he must have to live with. How do we fight the air of unreality that these things create around us? The feeling that we are all supposed to be here this morning and sit quietly while the preacher fulfills his assigned role? While he stands there for thirty minutes and says what he is expected to say?

How do we communicate when a great gulf is fixed between our minds and the hearers' minds? Being preachers, we have stuffed our minds with different baggage from theirs. If we have tried to fill our vision with God and His Word, we can barely hope that many of our people have made such an attempt. We have spent a good share of the past week studying the passage of Scripture, but many of our hearers may have trouble even finding it in their Bibles. The children in the pews might not listen at all, on the grounds that what matters to big people can hardly be important to little people. With different interests, different values, even different vocabularies, how can we shout across that gulf the truths and claims of God?

If the word "communicate" has become a jargon word, it still has some value to us. It speaks of a transfer or a sharing of ideas between minds. Usually it implies a two-way sharing. Preaching is mostly one-way, but we can still speak of it as communicating, just as a writer in a pastoral newsletter wrote of the editors of *Time* as being real communicators. So how do we communicate? How do we get ideas across?

Character

As mentioned on page 18, it was once a truism in artillery that a cannon had to weigh at least a hundred times as much as the shot it fired. In some sense a communicator has to weigh more than the message. He has to be someone worth listening to. It is this weight that we may call character.

Character comes on at least two levels. First, we may speak of force of character. This describes the speaker whose presence carries such command, such authority, that we have to listen. Force of character compels attention, apart from such integrity as the speaker may have. A preacher may be an unworthy man, but if something about him is intimidating, he may also be an able communicator. Force alone, however, endangers the preacher who has it, and for obvious spiritual reasons.

The second level of character is integrity. A preacher may be meek, but if he is real, he speaks from a position of strength. We may hope that such a man has finally committed himself to his ministry. We hope that his life is open to scrutiny, that his family life is a credit to the ministry and that he keeps his word and pays his debts. We hope that he is a model of what he preaches, that he forgives his enemies and that he remembers the towel around his waist.

Integrity has more than this negative side. It means that a person knows God and loves the Book, that he has a vital devotional life. There may be successful actors in the ministry, and they may be able communicators. But enough discerning Christians are around that even in this world the actors will be known for what they are. Lincoln's dictum will hold, which began, "You may deceive all of the people part of the time. . . ."

Habit

A second quality of a communicator is that he habitually works at communicating. It becomes a sort of holy grail to him, a life quest. He savors words, he likes ideas. He chafes when he is not filling his mind, reflecting on what is in his mind or else speaking his mind.

This goes with our tradition that a minister ought to own a library and that he ought to spend time reading it. Rumor once had it that Spurgeon read three or four heavy books a week, but then he was a lightning reader. On the other hand, a pastor was heard to say that he did not have time at all to read books. Somewhere between these extremes we all live and wish we had more time to read. At the least, we have to take specific time each day studying the Bible—and at least to live by the dictum, "No Bible, no breakfast."

If a communicator by habit keeps stocking his mind, he also finds ways to speak it. Not only that, he gets good at it.

Preparation

The first several chapters of this book told how to prepare a sermon. Preparing to communicate is almost a separate activity. If a sermon is going to get across, it has to have a firm base, a Scripturally logical outline. It also has to have good components: illustrations, explanations, arguments, applications that fit. So what lack we yet?

The chapter on imagination takes on new importance at this point. The casserole isn't done when you get the recipe and have all the ingredients laid out on the counter. The sermon preparation is not done even after you have assembled all the parts. At this stage a sermon may still be highly forgettable. The sermon you remember is generally the one whose preparation went beyond this point—the preacher prepared to communicate.

As you reflect on your new sermon outline and on the passage from which you got it, you can hope that something fresh will strike you. You pray over it. You visualize the historical setting, and you keep at it until your mind arrives at a fresh insight. In time that insight is almost sure to come; it is a sort of homiletical second work of grace. The passage may strike you with a new vividness, as though the scene opened to you in new colors and depth. The persons involved may take on a new reality. No longer storybook figures smaller than life, they take on flesh and breath, facing problems that correspond to our own. The passage may take on new urgency, as its life-and-death implications open out.

Or you may see the passage from a fresh angle, as when you first looked at the Prodigal Son through the cold eyes of the older brother or when you tried to look at Joseph's administration through the eyes of the Egyptians.

An effective preacher once told me that it helped him to meditate on the historical setting of the passage. He said that if he reflected long enough, this line of thought never failed to give him fresh insights into the passage he was working on.

If there is any caution to be observed here, it is that we not go too far. We have all heard brilliant inferences from Scripture, as when the late M. R. DeHaan described the way that the Lord restored Sarah's youth after she had passed the age of ninety. When two chapters later Abimelech took her into his royal household, can we imagine his wanting to marry a woman in tottering old age? The inference looks valid, and DeHaan made it memorable. On the other hand, we can remember sermons that went too far. They built a tissue of imagination and description that went so far beyond what the Scripture would bear that we felt uneasy. What may get printed in a historical novel is one thing. Pulpit dissonances are something else, and cultivated discernment at this point may judge how much is enough.

Determination

How much do we want to get it across? A communicator wants to communicate. He may have one or another motive for wanting to do this, but he does very much want to get his ideas across.

Some communicators seem driven by a compulsion to express themselves. They tend to hold the floor in conversation, and they write fluently. Speaking brings a kind of pleasure, and the conclusion brings release. Jeremiah wrote: "Then I said, I will not make mention of him, nor speak any more in his name. But his word was in mine heart as a burning fire shut up in my bones, and I was weary with forbearing, and I could not stay" (Jer. 20:9).

David gave almost the same sentiment in Psalm 39. So did the four lepers outside Samaria when they were taking the abandoned wealth of the Syrians: "Then they said one to another, We do not well: this day is a day of good tidings, and we hold our peace: if we tarry till the morning light, some mischief will come upon us: now therefore come, that we may go and tell the king's household" (2 Kings 7:9).

It may depend on the nature of the person, or it may depend on the importance of the message; but some preachers have fires burning in them that drive them to speak.

Some communicators are driven by a desire to impress. They live for the appreciation of an audience. The response becomes not only a spur to effective communication; it can be an intoxicant. Those of us who preach know something of what an appreciative audience can do for the preacher. We also know the numbing effect that a cold audience can have. Get the people comfortable, sitting close, laughing at our jokes, and soon we cannot do anything wrong. They respond to us, and they may even make eternal decisions at the invitation. The sermon becomes a two-way communication: the hearers encouraging the preacher and the preacher encouraging them. Heady stuff, and a powerful lift to a preacher's vanity, as well as a strong motive to communicate.

Paul dealt with this temptation when he wrote to the Galatians, "For do I now persuade men, or God? or do I seek to please men? for if I yet pleased men, I should not be the servant of Christ" (Gal. 1:10). Note how carefully he distinguished persuading from pleasing. He persuaded men; he sought to please God.

> For our exhortation was not of deceit, nor of uncleanness, nor in guile: but as we were allowed of God to be put in trust with the gospel, even so we speak; not as pleasing men, but God, which trieth our hearts. For neither at any time used we flattering words, as ye know, nor a cloak of covetousness; God is witness: nor of men sought we glory, neither of you, nor yet of others, when we might have been burdensome, as the apostles of Christ (1 Thess. 2:3–6).

The able communicator wants to get his ideas across. Love purposes the good of the beloved, and the true pastor purposes the good of his people. He is convinced of the urgency of his message, and he longs for the spiritual growth of his people. To the Ephesian elders Paul said,

Being a Communicator

> Ye know, from the first day that I came into Asia, after what manner I have been with you at all seasons, serving the Lord with all humility of mind, and with many tears, and temptations, which befell me by the lying in wait of the Jews: and how I kept back nothing that was profitable unto you, but have shewed you, and have taught you publickly, and from house to house, testifying both to the Jews, and also to the Greeks, repentance toward God, and faith toward our Lord Jesus Christ (Acts 20:18–21).

Whatever his motives, the communicator keeps thinking, "I'll make you understand." His determination helps him do it.

Manner

The truism seems self-evident that in order to get an idea across you must have it clearly in mind. If you are going to communicate your sermon, it had better be a good one. This means that it must not only convey the Bible passage; it should also be free from internal dissonances. If two of your main heads overlap, few of your hearers might be quick enough to explain how they overlap, but many of your hearers will sense that something is not quite right. If your sermon is going to get across, you will also have to make your transitions clear.

This is so important that it bears repeating. You have to make your transitions clear. Each main head needs to be distinct. Dr. Charles Koller used to say in class, "Every sermon needs a skeleton, but do not rattle the bones unduly." He was right; we do not help people much by talking about the outline itself. We do help people by enabling them to see each main division of our message. Keep each part in a separate package. Some men lower their voices and skim over the statement of the next main head, as though it were something artificial to be apologized for. They admit the statement as they might admit the name of a son now serving time in the state prison. For clarity's sake, the main divisions have to stand out, and the transitions have to be clear.

Not only does a communicator clarify, but he also converses. That is to say, the most effective platform speakers are those who speak as over a lunch table or in a living room. They are loud enough to reach their hearers; that is to say, they project. They may gesture more emphatically. But they do not sound like orators or train callers. They do not yell their sermons or shout or intone them. Their pattern is conversational. No hearer will ever have the impulse to say, "Aw, come off it."

94

If there is any real objection to this, it would probably come along one of two lines. First, does not the Bible word for "preach" mean "proclaim"? And, second, the great preachers of the past—were they not orators and proclaimers?

First, the common New Testament word for "preach" is *kerusso*. The eight or so other words either stress content or have neutral connotations. Of *kerusso* and *kerux*, the first connotation seems to involve a loud and resonant voice. The second seems to be that the speaker is publicly giving someone else's message. A third is that he speaks under divine protection, even authority. He may even speak for men to God. But go through Kittel's extended treatment of these words, and you come out with no necessary idea of the herald's speech pattern. He might be conveying the sense in a conversational pattern, or he might merely be pronouncing the words in a loud voice. The word *kerusso* occurs 61 times in the New Testament. While it often means to get ideas across, I find no usage that requires us to suppose that the herald had to intone or chant the message.

Second, it may well be that back through the years the effective preachers were more oratorical than this chapter seems to recommend. Read *The Metropolitan Tabernacle Pulpit* and try to imagine the power of Spurgeon's eloquence. Oratory? Perhaps, but it was surely direct communication. Read some of his conclusions and try to imagine that he was intoning them. In his *Lectures to His Students*, he said,

> You may go all round, to church and chapel alike, and you will find that by far the larger majority of our preachers have a holy tone for Sundays. They have one voice for the parlor and the bedroom, and quite another tone for the pulpit; so that if not double-tongued sinfully, they certainly are so literally. The moment some men shut the pulpit door, they leave their own personal manhood behind them, and become as official as the parish beadle. There they might almost boast with the Pharisee, that they are not as other men are, although it would be blasphemy to thank God for it.

Our present situation confronts us with its own problem. It is always true that effective platform speech talks directly. Each hearer feels that the speaker is talking to him. If this were true in earlier times, and I believe that it was, it is even more urgent now. Of those of us who preach, almost all are preaching to people nursed on television. The tube

Being a Communicator

is an intimate medium, and people are used to it. The Bible commands us to preach, so we preach. But how do we reconcile the principles of bold proclamation with conversational directness? Let us agree that we do not let our culture decide what the Bible tells us to do. Let us also agree that pulpit proclamation at its best does communicate, largely because it uses the patterns of conversation, not those of recitation.

QUESTIONS FOR DISCUSSION

1. Evaluate the statement that preaching is passé, that people need some intimate approach or they won't listen.

2. How can you help a person achieve a conversational pattern of delivery?

3. Of the well-known preachers of radio, television and the conference circuit, to what extent can they be called communicators? How do they do it?

4. How much can we learn from secular communicators?

5. Why does a dainty man have trouble communicating? Why are "holy tones" a hindrance?

6. At what point does a pulpit communicator reconcile pulpit oratory with the conversational pattern?

7. How much of communication involves talking to people in the second person, the "you" speaking directly to their own interests?

8. In comparison with "you," how well does "we" communicate?

9. What does pulpit communication have to do with passionate preaching? To what extent do they overlap?

CHAPTER 11

ANY CONCERN? ANY PASSION? ANY TEARS?

"I ceased not to warn every one night and day with tears" (Acts 20:31).

An old preacher described a noonday sermon he had heard during the time he was training for the ministry. Paul Rader was preaching in a downtown Chicago theater, and perhaps eleven hundred businessmen had packed the place out. Rader walked out on the stage and began to preach a simple salvation message. Soon tears were coursing down his face. After about twenty-five or thirty minutes he seemed to drop his arms, and he said, "Well, I've preached long enough. How many of you men would like to receive Christ this noon? Would you please stand up?" As if on springs, perhaps a hundred fifty, perhaps two hundred men stood. Rader said, "Please sit down again. I don't think I made it clear." And for another five minutes he went over the plan of salvation in his simplest terms. Then he repeated, "Would any of you still want to receive Christ? Would you please stand?" And again the same number of men rose to their feet.

It is possible to preach a relaxed sermon. The preacher talks about divine truth in a calm, even warm, manner, a manner wholly without intensity. Considering how many battered saints need some comfort, there has to be a case for a certain amount of low-voltage preaching. However, if a whole ministry lacks tears and intensity, might we not suppose that something Pauline is lacking? Is it possible that a man of God can handle the unsearchable riches of divine truth without being stirred himself? These days it would seem so.

It is possible to work up an emotional excitement for preaching, especially in those denominations and churches where people expect some sound and fury. Once a preacher has the habit or the mind-set, he can shout with less emotional effort than the gymnast or the weight lifter psyching himself up for his supreme effort. However, the example of Nadab and Abihu offering their strange fire should make us pause at any emotional intensity that springs from another altar than God's own. The holy anointing oil was not for man's flesh, and we can hardly hope that the Spirit of God will anoint any carnal attempts of our own with the power for which in our better moments we yearn.

It is possible to preach with force. In such a case the sermon comes across loud from an overbearing presence. The intensity does not seem to rise from a concern for people or for the truths being preached. Indeed, the preacher's face may show anger, but nothing like tears or passion. Again, it would appear that something Pauline is missing.

Several reasons might offer themselves for the calm and tearless preaching that seems to be increasingly widespread in circles that profess Biblical faith. One that we hear every so often is that a laid-back style has become fashionable. A whole generation schooled on television is used to an intimate medium, and therefore they feel easier listening to a man speaking across a desk. While this may have a certain plausibility, it is hard to find a Bible verse for such clinical detachment, especially when Paul told us to rejoice with them that do rejoice and weep with them that weep.

Possibly a more sinister reason may be in the way that attitudes have shifted in the last years. Over three decades ago, Dr. Harold C. Mason remarked in class that the trend seemed to be toward the suave Christ. While Mason was talking about the fashions in liberal church school materials, his prediction covered what would happen among evangelicals a generation later. We might find ways to confirm this. At the same time we seem to have a creeping universalism among those who profess the faith once delivered. It has become ever more difficult to believe in a literal Hell as described in Mark 9 and Revelation 20, and that the lost are actually going there. Even the word "lost" is now dated; one speaks of the "unchurched." In view of such attitudes, hard to document but still discernable, why should we not have a corresponding lowering of pulpit passion?

Awe of God

At the turn of the century, Henry C. Vedder noted several trends after a century of Baptist advance in the United States. One of these was that church membership was drawing increasingly on the Sunday School and less and less on adult conversions. The aftermath of what he saw is what we live with. Many of us were saved in childhood in Christian homes and are third-, fourth-, even fifth-generation Christians. While we can praise the Lord for every sinner who repents, whatever his age, a result is a Christian community in which comparatively few of us have the wonder of God that comes from an adult conversion.

An assembly line worker with a rugged life made a clear profession of faith. About two months later his fellow workers were teasing him about his religion. One asked, "I suppose you believe that stuff about Jesus turning the water into wine?"

"I don't know about that, but He sure turned beer into furniture."

With preachers who seem mostly to have professed Christ when they were children, is it any great surprise if we tend to preach with no great passion? We are tempted to take God for granted, much as we presume on electric power and the availability of groceries and gasoline. From childhood we have had to memorize Bible verses and choruses. We took doctrine and Bible stories in Sunday School. Somewhere along the line we learned the attributes of God. At two or three sermons a week, we may have had to sit through more than two thousand sermons before we went away to college. "All these have I kept from my youth up. What lack I yet?" Any wonder that when it comes to eternal things, some of us do not have much to marvel about. And without that wonder, how can we rightly preach the unsearchable riches? But with that wonder, can we not hope for something contagious in our preaching?

If we are going to preach with passion, it would seem that much of that passion will come from our own experience with God. It is one thing to get an outline on John 3:16. It is something else to feel the saving power of God on a person. It is one thing to get a homiletical outline from 2 Corinthians 1. It is something else to face grief with the conviction that God's loving hand is still on us.

A veteran pastor had in his church a boy who broke his arm. After a long and painful healing, the boy hardly had his cast off before he broke it all over again. That night in his hospital room he lay in his bed hurting and discouraged, with his parents and his pastor standing by. His pastor asked him softly, "Does God love you?"

After a pause, "Yes, He does."

"Is God good?"

Through tears, "Yes, He is."

At that moment the boy's faith had to rest on something else than his experience, but on the basis of Scripture it became real in his experience.

Any Concern?

To the extent that God is real in our experience, we can hope to preach Him with passion and concern. Peter said, "For we cannot but speak the things which we have seen and heard" (Acts 4:20). A. W. Tozer once said that a scribe tells something he read somewhere, but a prophet tells something he heard. Whether God saved us in our childhood or after a life of sin, we still have to meet Him experientially and daily, and then our preaching is bound to show Him in our warmth and zeal.

In John 17:3 Jesus linked eternal life with knowing God. Paul so yearned to know Christ that he was willing to renounce every asset that he had in order to enter into acquaintance with Him (Phil. 3:7–14). Have we now come to the place where such a religion is too costly? Are we more comfortable with a religion that takes the Bible only as a textbook, that requires assent to a sound doctrinal statement and that assures us of Heaven forever, by faith in a God we need not meet daily? Any wonder that while some men are proclaiming the Cross, others are coolly moralizing on clothes, hair lengths, Thursday night visitation and religious pop psychology? When Jesus yielded up His spirit, the veil was rent in twain from top to bottom in a building some men have no thought of entering, to open an immediate communion they do not seem to want, much less commend to their congregations. We have the high privilege of access into the Awesome Presence and of acquaintance with the Eternal. To paraphrase John 16:27, "For the Father Himself regards you with warm affection, because you have settled your warm affection on Me and have rested your faith in the fact that I came out from God."

If we can undertake those spiritual activities that deepen our wonder at God, can we not suppose that we will preach with a deeper urgency and passion? Because if we do not, our preaching is going to sound tinny to the discerning among our hearers.

Love for the Bible

David said, "O how love I thy law! it is my meditation all the day" (Ps. 119:97). Jesus said to the Jews who believed on Him, "If ye continue in my word, then are ye my disciples indeed" (John 8:31). May it be true that every person who reads this can look at his Bible, fondle its cover and feel from his heart, "I love this book." May he love it because it is indeed the Word of God.

Probably our observation will bear out the fact that love for the Lord

100

goes with a love for His book. Can you name an acquaintance you believe to have a vital fellowship with God but who does not treasure his Bible? Or a true lover of Scripture who takes the Lord casually? If either type actually exists, he must be rare.

Not that the world we live in is any help. We may suppose that the flesh always takes a detached view of Holy Writ. How much more in a century of relativism, in which there are no fixed values; of humanism, in which man is the measure of all things; of materialism, in which things are all that matter; and of rationalism, in which the human mind is supposed to be able to solve all problems. Even among believers can we not detect a creeping acceptance of the world's values and a disposition to feel apologetic about the Lord and His book? "Is this vile world a friend to grace, to help me on to God?" Do not many professing Christians take the Bible in about the same casual way that the bereaved harlot regarded the other woman's baby (1 Kings 3:26)?

But to the preacher who loves the Bible, will he not feel emotional about it? And will not that emotion often overflow in passion for given verses and doctrines? Can we ever feel detached about the inspiration and inerrancy of Scripture? Can we ever take the attributes of God casually? Do we ever wholly lose our wonder at the redemptive program? If we had no other cause for passion, even for tears in our sermons, the Bible itself ought to generate passion and even tears.

Two seminary couples had supper together. On the way home one man said to his wife, "My friend back there will never succeed in the ministry."

"What makes you say that?"

"Because he doesn't love the Word of God."

Two decades have borne out his prediction.

Concern for People

"But we were gentle among you, even as a nurse cherisheth her children: so being affectionately desirous of you, we were willing to have imparted unto you, not the gospel of God only, but also our own souls, because ye were dear unto us" (1 Thess. 2:7, 8).

It was Kant who remarked that virtue consists in loving people and using things. Whenever a preacher reverses these, his ministry is in trouble, no matter what statistics he can show. When he loves his people and refuses to love things, something has to be right about his ministry.

Any Concern?

We may well ask, How much do we feel the awful destiny of the lost? God may find a way to pardon our occasional annoyance at the behavior of the unsaved; but He may go harder on our unwillingness to believe Revelation 20:15. A sort of creeping universalism is something we not only discern; probably we could document it. Granted that we tend to get discouraged after just so many failed attempts to lead unsaved people to Christ. But if we appreciate the holiness of God, and if we let our imaginations work on what it is like to be in Hell, we will surely view lost persons with different eyes and will preach to them with different urgency. We will care for them more than they care about themselves. To be sure, all men have not faith. Many of them want to be with the laughing crowd. They loathe the thought of being in a prayer meeting. For them surely the gates of Hell are locked on the inside.

But what of the lost who loathe themselves and live in misery—the wretched, the losers, the jaded survivors? A successful pastor asked a fellow pastor what he did when people like that came into his services. The reply he got ought to chill any of us: "I get rid of them the quickest way I can."

But what of the losers and the jaded—the repeatedly divorced, the desolate, the guilt-ridden homosexuals, the abandoned and the bored? Of such types God assembled a thriving church in Corinth, and can we not trust that there are yet ways to find them and preach to them with passion and hope?

On the other hand, what of our own members? How many of us have sat on the platform ready to preach and looked at the faces of our people, whose smiles covered all sorts of heartaches? Young people in the back rows, whispering to one another, in a world of their own, in various stages of alienation from the parents sitting farther forward? Parents who honestly tried to rear their children to follow Christ, and hardly a couple but have a rebellious son or daughter in debauchery or headed for it? Widows, lonely people, failures, some in constant pain—make your own list. The last thing they need on a given Sunday morning is a sermon cluttered with relationships, aspects, phases and abstractions. They need a loving Lord, and they need a caring preacher to proclaim Him.

In a fair number of churches the back of the pulpit bears words hidden from the congregation but speaking to whoever is on the platform: "Sir, we would see Jesus." We may wonder what earnest souls have painted them there.

Indignation Against Evil

"For all the people wept, when they heard the words of the law" (Neh. 8:9).

"Abhor that which is evil; cleave to that which is good" (Rom. 12:9).

At the outset of Jesus' earthly ministry, and again at the final week of it, He cleansed the temple. "The zeal of thine house hath eaten me up." In the synagogue His enemies "planted" a man with a withered hand, hoping to catch Jesus in the act of performing a healing work on the Sabbath Day. Mark noted that He looked on them with anger, being grieved for the hardness of their hearts (Mark 3:5). Most anger may be sin, but there is such a thing as the right kind, and Jesus had it. The Bible does not often commend grief, but Jesus had the right kind of that.

Paul commanded us to abhor that which is evil and to glue ourselves to what is good. In this sophisticated era, we seem to pride ourselves on being nonjudgmental in regard to people, and rightly so. It would seem, however, that at the same time we have become tolerant of sin itself, at least in those cases when it injures anyone but ourselves. Indeed, almost any overt act or statement against wickedness will prompt some fellow Christian to accuse us of overreacting. He might apply the same word to the punishment of Nadab, Korah, Achan or Eli. By this view Paul overreacted when he wrote 1 Corinthians 5.

Some of our toleration must have begun with our acceptance of the media. The truth holds that if you look at sin long enough, it will begin to look right. With a generation of Christians who have contemplated prime-time sin for as long as most of them can remember, is it any wonder there seems to be a pervasive tolerance of the sin around us? Even the serious magazines print words and graphics that were not printable a generation ago. What we once regarded as revolting has begun to take on redeeming social value. And we seem to take our tolerance for granted and even take some pride in it.

Once on a nearly deserted beach my wife and I learned something about what Paul meant in Philippians 3:2, "Beware of dogs." We were letting our dog run, and he came up to a fish house. The ripe odors that repelled us did not bother him at all; they fascinated him. Viewing our dog in terms of this verse, we realized that a certain type of person can bear any stench, any revolting situation, with calm, even fascination. Of such persons Paul said "Beware." We dare not permit ourselves to grow calloused toward evil. We guard our compassion. In the counseling room

Any Concern?

we keep ourselves unshockable, when at the same moment we inwardly groan at the dreary sins we didn't want to hear about.

If we are going to preach with passion, it would seem that we need to feel something of God's revulsion at sin, even while we try to keep our charity and compassion. God expects His prophets to take the strong view.

> Woe unto them that call evil good, and good evil; that put darkness for light, and light for darkness; that put bitter for sweet, and sweet for bitter! (Isa. 5:20).
>
> I have seen also in the prophets of Jerusalem an horrible thing: they commit adultery, and walk in lies: they strengthen also the hands of evildoers, that none return from his wickedness: they are all of them unto me as Sodom, and the inhabitants thereof as Gomorrah (Jer. 23:14).
>
> Her priests have violated my law, and have profaned mine holy things: they have put no difference between the holy and profane, neither have they showed difference between the unclean and the clean, and have hid their eyes from my sabbaths, and I am profaned among them (Ezek. 22:26).

To fulfill the intent of these passages, probably our greatest need is to keep short accounts with God. If we practice confessing our sins, He is faithful and righteous to forgive us on the spot. The habit of early confession must surely be a first step toward loathing our sins in any constructive sort of way and toward getting some measure of practical victory over them. A second need, and I know of no way to put these in order, is to seek Him in vital experience (Phil. 3:10). Isaiah saw the vision of God, and suddenly his sin took on a new horror to him. "Woe is me! for I am undone; because I am a man of unclean lips, and I dwell in the midst of a people of unclean lips: for mine eyes have seen the King, the LORD of Hosts" (Isa. 6:5).

Our third need fits what has already appeared in this chapter, a daily time in the Word of God. We can hardly know His mind apart from His Word. We can hardly hope to feel His revulsion at sin if we clutter our minds with all sorts of images instead of Scripture. How many people have written in how many Bibles, "Sin will keep you from this Book, or this Book will keep you from sin."

Have we any concern? Have we any passion? Have we any tears?

QUESTIONS FOR DISCUSSION

1. Some preachers are just not overly emotional. Should we expect them to work up passions that are not really their own?

2. Does this chapter account for the widespread lack of passion in preaching?

3. What would have to happen in our schools to reverse the trend? What generates Holy Spirit concern in a student preacher?

4. Cannot our schools train their students to preach with force? Must we insist on genuine feelings?

CHAPTER 12

IMAGINATION IN PREACHING

Imagination is not quite the same as freshness, and neither of them is the same as originality; but all three are close. All three involve the mind's ability to come up with something new. The word imagination brings to mind images of the genius in the garret, toiling by candlelight to think up original ideas, creation out of nothing. Actually, a psychologist friend was close to the truth when he said that every original idea you ever had is a case of your not being able to remember where you got it.

How does imagination work? By putting two or more familiar ideas together in a new combination. Regarding MacDonald's remark that Jesus never thought of being original, He must have sounded highly original to both the crowds and the disciples. Why not? Even though you can find Old Testament foundations for the Sermon on the Mount, it came in fresh combinations and in terms of heart obedience. To hearers used to externalism in their religion, these ideas must have sounded like nothing they had ever heard before.

Do we strive for originality for its own sake? Lewis at the last page of *Mere Christianity* was doubtless correct when he remarked that originality comes when we strive for something else. If we strive for mere novelty, we will almost surely injure our communication. If on the other hand we strive to put truth in the clearest way possible, we will come across to our hearers as original and imaginative. It is in this light that we need to see the rest of this chapter.

So what is it going to take for us to preach with imagination and originality?

A Full Mind

To have a full mind does not depend on how long you live, or the elderly would be the most creative people we know. It is *how* you live. Much of imagination must draw on childhood experience, or else it must be caught from an observant parent or teacher who taught how to perceive. The child who lives among books probably has an advantage,

Imagination in Preaching

learning to value what he cannot even use yet. In any case, the beginning of imagination would seem to be a full mind. The more you have in your memory bank, the more your mind has to work with. We may wonder if the full mind comes from a series of acts or from a way of life, but the two go together. The chain of acts makes for a way of life. After finishing seminary, a graduate wrote to another member of that class. His key question was, "What books are you reading these days?"—a vital concern to preachers; and "he being dead yet speaketh." We each need a full mind.

To have a full mind, any of us could make his own list. It would probably come out close to this:

1. Faithful and intensive Bible study.
2. Regular reading of the books in our libraries—Biblical, theological, devotional and other. Books dealing with specific problems we may face. Literature. History.
3. Current periodicals, somehow.
4. Daily newspaper. A former professor advised us to read the paper standing up so that we could keep up on the news without wasting too much time.
5. Intelligent conversation. Not all conversation is intelligent. Each of us knows a few people who either are loaded with current information or who have a marvelous effect on our own thinking. With them conversation majors on ideas and events, little on people. Their friendship is worth gold, and they mentally stimulate us.
6. Formal education, which overlaps all of these. It is supposed to help them all, and often it does.
7. Living itself. Some of us live sheltered lives, ministering to our own people in familiar situations. Some of us don't even know what is going on within the confines of our own church buildings. Others spend faithful time with the books and still make life a series of zestful encounters. They easily strike up conversations with strangers. They ride in ambulances or turn up in police stations after midnight. They find ways to pick people's brains. They are curious about many things, and they have a way of getting into odd situations—to them all life is a learning process. They get into factories and offices and have coffee with people who work there.

Our former landlady was talking with a craggy-looking old friend of hers. "Jake, we graduated from school together, but look at you now! Nobody would ever think we were the same age."

He answered, "Yes, Millicent, but I've lived."

Models of Imaginative Thinking

While it helps to have a full mind, imaginative thinking involves using it, doing something fresh, putting familiar ideas together to get new combinations, new ideas. It helps to watch others who are good at it. Since we are preachers, it helps us to hear or read sermons that show some real effort at clarity. If a sermon gets into print, it was probably because an editor needed it to fill space or because he saw something unique in it. Printed sermons then have a fair chance of suggesting how someone got fresh insights. You probably have your own favorites. On a friend's recommendation I bought some works of George H. Morrison, a Scottish preacher of the last century, and I find him particularly inspiring.

A preacher was about to begin his message when he produced an egg and called his wife to the platform. He explained that many families in the church had young children and that the life and the mind of a little child are fragile. (They had one of their own.) With what care parents need to treat that fragile life! He then tossed the egg to his wife. Each took a step back. She tossed the egg to him. Again a step back. He tossed it to her. Another step back. She tossed it to him. The last toss was the length of the platform. With the egg somehow still intact, he dismissed his wife and remarked about the care with which each family was rearing its children. "Then we send him off to school—" and he tossed the egg over his shoulder to smash somewhere in the choir loft.

With that introduction he had little trouble holding his people's interest as he preached about rearing children.

Specific Prayer

A college chapel speaker once remarked that prayer is the greatest time-saver in the world. He surely was right. If we specifically ask God to give us fresh insights into a passage, it is the sort of prayer for which we can trust for an answer, and probably soon.

One of the ministries of the Holy Spirit is to recall things to our attention, especially the things Jesus said (John 14:26). He may favor us with an extension of this reminding ministry, as when we prayed for help with examinations. Can we not trust that when we pray, He will enable us to make use of the vast amount of material stored in our minds, but much of it beyond recall? Doubtless this is the sort of help that He delights to give. As we pray, we can hope that He will work in our minds, both to deepen our understanding of the passage and to give us fresh understanding of how to convey that passage to others.

Reflection

This step takes work. A certain amount of it takes place when we do routine work, such as mowing a lawn or driving. We do a certain amount of reflection unconsciously. Some insights come after concentration and then a time gap. We seem to do some reflecting in our sleep, and bedtime review has a way of getting our minds to work during the night. Study just before bedtime has a wonderful payoff because it leads to that sort of reflection. Then there is the reflection that takes specific work.

Probably our most productive reflection is what we make ourselves do. Take time to stare at a passage. As you continue reading and rereading it, note how you observe what you hadn't seen during the first reading or even the sixth. Words show up in a fresh light. Sequences appear, and you begin counting things. You think of parallel passages. You sense what are the stressed words. Sentence structure takes on new meaning. You get curious about the force of the original, and you list words and names that you want to look up. You look at the passage through different eyes—how does God view this? How did the writer view it? How did the persons in the event regard it? For example, how did Jacob's view contrast with Laban's? How did Barnabas's view compare with Paul's? How might the first hearers have felt about a given epistle when they first heard it read to them?

Just as you make yourself observe, you make yourself question. You look at your outline, and you begin to ask such questions as

1. Is this what the Bible really intends?
2. Is this the best way to express it?
3. What does this outline do to help people remember it?
4. What is unique about it? How much of it looks like stock parts out of the bin?
5. How many of these ideas have I preached lately?
6. What is here to arouse curiosity?
7. Could I find some sort of visual aid that would help this?

8. To what basic motivation does this appeal?

As you concentrate, your mind works. The insights may take a while to come, but they will come. The more you concentrate on the inquiry, the more fresh ideas you seem to harvest.

You try to remember the forgotten name of a remote acquaintance. Intense concentration fails to recall it—for the time being. Several hours, perhaps a day later, your mind by some marvelous process traces it down. By ways that may baffle us, the mind has the power to trace ideas and regroup them into fresh combinations; but it does most of this work only after we have gone to some effort to feed our request into it.

Freshness

When it comes to fresh sermon material, how much should we demand of ourselves? Most of us would agree that much material in the Bible lends itself to preaching, but we have not preached it yet. If an expositor were to set himself to preach a whole chapter of the Bible each Sunday morning, another on Sunday night and yet another in his midweek service, he would take eight years to preach through the Bible. A textual preacher would take fifty years to preach through the New Testament alone.

Many of us seem to leave great portions of the Bible unpreached. The historic books take up almost half the Bible, but most of them we rarely treat. Some of us preach from the poetic books, but rarely exhaustively. Of the major prophets, how much of Isaiah do we hear but the Christmas passages, plus chapters 6, 40 and 53? What do our people know of Jeremiah except some vague idea that he spent time in a pit and wept? Or of Ezekiel—did he deal with anything other than the watchman, standing in the gap and the destiny of Russia? At least Daniel probably gets more attention. Of the Minor Prophets, who gets preached but Jonah, and Malachi's words about bringing the tithes into the storehouse?

Let us grant that in preaching the Old Testament we have at least two problems. First, many passages do not present themselves for exposition. The genealogies have their place in the divine order, but other passages strike us to have greater pulpit urgency. Certain passages, especially in Leviticus and the Prophets, we simply find hard to preach, and this in no way implies a low view of inspiration. Second, we need to divide the Word of Truth to discern what Old Testament material applied only to Israel, and what is eternal truth, applying to God's people of all the ages in the sweep of history.

Let us admit that Scripture has much material that we have not yet preached but need to preach.

Is it Biblical to repeat a sermon? The Synoptics suggest that Jesus repeated ideas and parables, if not whole sermons. Luke 6 includes material found in the Sermon on the Mount, but it is not the same sermon. Acts 13 seems to give Paul's standard approach his first time in a given synagogue. Verse 42 says that the Gentiles asked him to preach it again the following week. Luke does not say that he actually did.

Whether the prophets and teachers repeated their sermons, we can believe that they never sounded stale.

Should we repeat sermons? A collection of old outlines gives us a strong temptation to preach some of them over again. For the traveling evangelist the pressure is strong indeed, when real time for study can be an uncommon luxury. For the pastor who has been a long time in a church, almost the only time he can safely repeat a sermon is when he is away from his own pulpit. Most congregations seem to prefer fresh sermons, and when someone hears a preacher give the same sermon a second time, some respect tends to drain away. For the pastor in the enviable position of needing to have more than one morning service, he may well preach the same sermon in both services. However, he will probably find few people from the early service attending the later one to hear the sermon over again. This should give us a clue as to how much our people like to have a sermon repeated. Usually even the organist slips out of the second service.

The approach to sermon preparation that this book recommends may seem rigid and demanding; but once a person grasps it, he finds that most passages open easily to him. I have heard repeated testimonies from men who have learned how to outline—that organizing often becomes almost effortless. They still need time for exegesis first and for finishing later, but it is often easier to prepare a fresh outline than to revitalize an old one.

Some passages cry out to be preached over and over, such as 1 John 1:9. Even if we find it necessary to repeat these burdens every few months, we can at least pray enough and study enough that the repeated message comes across with a fresh outline, fresh illustrations, fresh insights and fresh urgency.

Some preachers are known to rail at their wives for serving left-overs. Not so often do we hear them disapprove of serving pulpit left-overs.

We do well to make it a life goal to preach a fresh message every time we preach.

The Introduction

Of all the points at which a sermon needs an imaginative approach, probably the introduction is the most important. If the introduction limps, an emotional illustration later might retrieve interest, but the real point of the sermon is not likely to get across. And how many introductions limp! A stock approach is to settle on some word in the theme, say the word "inventory." The preacher begins his sermon by telling his memories of the job he once had in a hardware store and of the week he helped to take inventory. After several minutes he moves to the subject of taking spiritual inventory of our lives, and he is into the body of his sermon. The introduction turned out to have little to do with the message, but it at least provided a diving board from which to jump in.

Another stock approach, and probably a better one, is to read the text passage and to explain its historical background. A preacher can easily find the material in his reference books, and it will probably be fresh to every member of his congregation. If he tells it with animation, it should generate interest for what is to come. A stock approach, true, but usually a good one. Yet there may be better ways.

A certain preacher once began by asking his people to imagine themselves at a track meet. The runners are getting ready for the hundred-yard dash. While they flex and warm up, another runner comes to join them. This last is a man of about five-foot-five, weighing about 270 pounds. He is wearing an overcoat, mittens, a fur hat, huge rubber boots and an enormous backpack. There he is, smiling and lumbering up to the starting line. Anyone want to guess how he makes the first fifteen yards, let alone finishes the race?

Now quickly change the scene. You're out in a boat, and somehow you tip out of it. While you get a lung full of water, the boat floats away out of reach. You struggle to the surface and call "Help!" And sure enough, on the dock a city block away, is Mister Five-Foot-Five, pack and all. He calls out, "Hang on! I'm coming!"—and prepares to dive in. What chance do you give him of swimming out and getting you to shore?

Imagination in Preaching

Now, the preacher went on, you may be the only one standing between your neighbors and the Lake of Fire. I ask you, what do they see? A Christian stripped for the race? Or do they see a person loaded down with weights? Thereupon he read his text, Hebrews 12:1 and 2.

Another time the same preacher opened by reading the story of Pilate and what sounded like a stock sermon on "What will you do with Jesus?" Suddenly it became evident that he was not going that way. He was stressing that Pilate wanted to do the right thing; repeatedly he tried to get Jesus off. "I find no fault in this man." However, as soon as Pilate realized that it was going to cost him something, he reluctantly caved in. The sermon had to do with moral courage. What seemed to begin as a cliché turned out to be a pulpit blockbuster.

What then should an introduction do? Obviously, it should prepare the people for the sermon. It should get their attention and awaken their interest. It should fit the sermon. A pertinent story helps more than five jokes, and it has the advantage of leading easily into an exposition of Holy Scripture. What five jokes can make that claim? In addition the introduction should lead easily to the proposition. Ideally the introduction should stir up some feeling for the sermon, rather as Nathan did in 2 Samuel 12.

How long should the introduction be? By any standard of balance and fitness it should be proportionate to the length of the sermon. One night a great preacher discoursed on atomic energy. After an hour he remarked that that was his introduction; the body of his sermon took another twenty minutes, and the whole thing was fascinating enough that probably nobody minded. Few of the rest of us could carry it off at all. A pastor of mine once preached half an hour on the three sisters: grace, mercy and peace (2 Tim. 1:2). Afterward when I thanked him for his good message, he confided that it was all his introduction, that he never did get to his sermon. Well, not bad. Great pulpit man that he is, he could do it and end up ahead.

So much for the brilliant exceptions. For the rest of us, ten lines are too little and ten minutes are too much. Somewhere within those limits we ought to find enough to say to intrigue our people. The real problem, however, is not how much we say, but how well we engage interest. This brings us back to the subject of imagination. How can we find fresh means to express familiar truths and fresh ways to convey them?

How can we entice people to God?

QUESTIONS FOR DISCUSSION

1. What is the distinction between imagination, originality and freshness?

2. Why is imagination a sort of by-product and not an end in itself? In what quest does imagination come?

3. Evaluate the media for their part in encouraging or discouraging originality.

4. What is the relation between imagination and a full mind?

5. What are the marks of a good introduction? Just how do you set about to get a good one?

6. What does imagination have to do with pulpit passion?

CHAPTER 13

HOW DOES SUGGESTION WORK?

Those who believe in the importance of preaching do well to study principles of suggestion. For getting ideas across, few subjects are more important; and as preachers, we do well not to permit ourselves to be ignorant of this field. For one thing, persuasion is largely a matter of suggestion; and suggestion is a powerful tool for getting ideas across, for imparting values and for influencing actions. Suggestion is the true stuff of advertising, and whether we are conscious of it or not, it is also the stuff of our ministries. Suggestion is either helping our work or hindering it, and we need to know how this mechanism works. For example, how many religious people tell of learning new sins in the confessional, when the priest asked about sins they had not yet thought of committing? Furthermore, a knowledge of suggestion will help us analyze those situations in which suggestion is being used to manipulate us. Knowledge is power, and such knowledge will make us less vulnerable in a world that is bombarding us with all sorts of ideas, most of which seem to come from the pit.

At the outset let it be understood that the whole subject has profound ethical implications. Good men and evil men plant ideas; but we hate to think that good men manipulate others. That is why this chapter needs to be read with reflection and discernment, not only that you might protect yourself and your people from the clever, but that you might make wise and right use of these principles yourself.

The whole study of suggestion begins with two concepts. First, ideas are dynamic and tend to express themselves in action. You see this easily in children. The little boy has a bean in his hand. He is looking at it intently. Whatever might be in his mind, you tell him not to push that bean up his nose. What does he do with the bean? Your own reflection should recall instances that illustrate the concept.

Second, ideas can be planted, as in the above example. All the imagination of the advertising industry works to think of different ways to plant them. The only teacher I ever had who dealt with this subject did a commentary on Marc Antony's funeral oration. In a situation in which the conspirators might kill him at any moment, Antony planted idea after idea. He wound it up by taking out Caesar's will; then he put it away again. The crowd cried out to hear the will. Antony responded that he could not read the will and that if he read the will, they would burn the houses of the conspirators. He then let them persuade him to read the will, and the scene ended with the crowd rushing off to carry out the idea that Antony had planted. Neat.

A pastor once told what happened when he asked prayer of a church he once had served. He was at the time interviewing for another position, and he asked his church to pray for God's will whether he should continue as their pastor. Is it any great wonder that his very prayer request planted an idea that was bound to ferment in many minds? And that that idea expressed itself in action? He *had* to find another church. Ideas can be planted, wittingly or unawares.

About the year 1939 there were hints that Franklin D. Roosevelt might run for a third term. Even Democrats recoiled in distaste at the thought of anyone seeking what not even George Washington had presumed to accept. Soon the Republicans began speaking against a third term, and they said it so often that the idea became commonplace; it was barely an issue when the real campaigning began. It had lost all of its shock value, even though the suggestions were planted to oppose a third term.

Pastors have wisely used the principle, as one did when he wanted his people to get interested in foreign missions. He had found himself leading a church that showed zero interest in missionary support. So every Sunday for about a year he made sure that he had at least one good missionary illustration in one of his sermons. At the end of the year, it seemed almost natural to the members to begin taking on missionaries and to make substantial commitments to their support. "As deceivers, yet true."

Many of our triumphs are intuitive. You start your service on time with zest and expectancy, and you convey something. You smile confidently, and that conveys something. You put out a neat, correctly worded bulletin, and that too conveys something. You quietly get rid of litter and the pasteboard boxes someone left in the hall. All these become effective and honest uses of suggestion. All these suggestions convey something positive, even dynamic, about your church. Conversely, the reverse of all these suggestions plants an opposing impression, chiefly that the church does not take its mission seriously.

Direct and Indirect Suggestion

The distinction here is important. Direct suggestion simply asks the desired response: Better buy Buick. Drink Coca-Cola. Donate blood. Let's eat out. Come forward while we sing. Direct suggestion is what you use when you are in control of the situation or when you need an immediate response.

Indirect suggestion only hints at the desired response. It plants the seed of an idea and lets the hearers reap it later on. For example, Paul wrote 2 Corinthians to a church that had all but rejected him. The Judaizers had made numbers of complaints against him, many having to do with his appearance and his height. Unlike them, he must have been short. He answered them in 10:12–14,

> For we dare not make ourselves of the number, or compare ourselves with some that commend themselves: but they measuring themselves by themselves, and comparing themselves among themselves, are not wise. But we will not boast of things without our measure, but according to the measure of the rule which God hath distributed to us, a measure to reach even unto you. For we stretch not ourselves beyond our measure, as though we reached not unto you: for we are come as far as to you also in preaching the gospel of Christ.

What is Paul saying here? That the proper measure of a missionary is not how tall he stands in cubits, but how far in miles he has succeeded in pioneering the gospel. However, that is not all. Between the lines he is saying much more. Indirect suggestion only hints at the ideas being planted.

As direct suggestion seeks an immediate response, indirect suggestion plants an idea in such a way that it can hope to get an eventual response. Direct suggestion is for an open audience; indirect is for a skeptical or hostile audience. Try leafing through the current copy of a major news magazine to note the primary impact of the ads. See if you do not find that few directly suggest that you buy the product; perhaps the Red Cross told you directly to donate blood, but note how the majority of the ads involve an indirect approach. It either presents the company name in cognitive dissonance ("What isn't changing at the Bell System") or speaks to some desire or curiosity ("Pleasure is where you find it," or "It's more than a convertible").

Years ago a leading news magazine printed a report of a hearing on gun control. With the article were pictures of two supposed witnesses at the hearing. In favor of gun control was a pretty, well-dressed, earnest-looking woman. Against control was an overweight, scowling, coarse-looking man. There was no appreciable slant in the article; there did not need to be. The pictures did it all with a powerful piece of indirect suggestion. It is not our way of planting an idea.

Let us then consider some Biblical examples. Compare Acts 2 with Acts 17. At Pentecost as Peter spoke to the curious throng, despite his repeated accusations of Israel's sin, he seemed plainly in control. "Ye men of Israel, hear these words." With the miracle, the apostles standing side by side and the Holy Spirit at work, the audience became increasingly polarized and pulled the conclusion out of Peter: "Men and brethren, what shall we do?" Peter answered, "Repent, and be baptized every one of you." Three thousand responded.

It was a different situation in Acts 17. Paul faced the skeptics of Athens, and it is difficult to believe that he spoke in the flesh (Acts 17:16, "His spirit was stirred in him"). With any wrong word he could have lost them in a moment. Note how he used mainly indirect suggestion. At last his mention of the Resurrection turned them off, and they left laughing. But he still had at least four believers. The hints in Paul's message make a study, but we find nothing like Peter's "Repent, and be baptized." (Some Bible students have used 1 Corinthians 2:1–5 to say that Paul used the wrong approach at Athens. If one of these critics were to preach at, say, Harvard, what is the probability that he could get at least four solid professions of faith?)

Negative Suggestion

This says some form of "Don't." Don't delay. Don't think that I'm after your job. You do trust me, don't you? Or the classic, "I'm not a crook." Negative suggestion is common among us, as in announcements that add, "Now you may feel that we're being tough about this, but that's not so."

Negative suggestion proposes its own counter. It plants the exact idea that it tries to head off. When someone says, "Don't cry," the one hurt may not yet have felt like crying. Airports do not often have machines offering flight insurance; why plant the negative idea that your plane might crash? In a tense meeting a deacon said to his pastor, "Now I'm not suggesting that you resign. . . ." Yet by these words he introduced a new idea, and whether he intended it or not, he was indeed suggesting that the pastor resign. The caution here is that any time we use words such as, "Now don't suppose that—" we had better be sure that we are not proposing a damaging idea that they would not have thought up without our help.

Countersuggestion

You will encounter situations in which you are bound to be opposed, no matter what. In these cases, countersuggestion may be a last resort: proposing the reverse of what you really want. You have surely had the experience of trying to persuade a negative mind of something, and all the while you were talking you had the feeling that he was barely listening. His mind was thinking up ways to say no. Then you changed your approach to, "You're not going to like this idea," or "You will see real problems in what I'm going to suggest," and he became receptive, finally.

As a manipulative device, countersuggestion is suspect. As a conversational means of prying open a negative mind, let us believe that it can be ethically justified. In a chapter on suggestion, it at least deserves some mention.

The Polarized Audience

If the ultimate degree of suggestion is hypnosis, then the last step before that degree is polarization. The audience as a group becomes highly suggestible, giving almost a knee-jerk response to whatever the speaker asks. In this situation the speaker stands in high esteem with the audience. The hearers are usually close together; polarization takes place usually in packed rooms or dense crowds. Young audiences polarize more easily than mature ones.

Your memory should recall such situations. The speaker had almost electric contact with his audience. They accepted his ideas without question; they hung on his words; they did what he told them to. Next day they might individually reconsider everything, but for the moment of encounter, at least, the speaker had power over them.

The phenomenal responses to some of the sermons in Acts give the impression of some polarized audiences, notably in the dense crowds of Pentecost and on Solomon's Porch (Acts 2, 3), and possibly in Cornelius's house, where Peter enjoyed immense prestige. The synagogue sermons of 13:16–41 and 14:1 may possibly have gone to polarized audiences, as well as Paul's long message to the disciples at Troas—despite the fall of Eutychus.

For more recent examples, Whitefield seemed often to have polarized his audiences, and Edwards must have achieved it at Enfield with his famous "Sinners in the Hands of an Angry God." Finney in his crest years of 1827–1832 apparently did it often, as did Henry Ward Beecher, at Plymouth Church, Brooklyn.

What if we realize that our audience has suddenly become just that suggestible? We need somehow to caution ourselves that polarization is no proof of Holy Spirit power over a group. Circumstances and charisma can bring it about by themselves. Indeed, a man can do it easier by means of a shrewd grasp of human nature than by agonizing nights with God.

Should we even try to polarize our hearers? A few rare preachers have such charisma that they often gain that level of attention. For the rest of us, it may well be a question of motive. Why does a person want people to respond so avidly to him? It is also a question of trust; is he leaning on the Spirit of God for results, or is he exploiting his knowledge of human nature by using psychological tricks?

The Media

Of the manipulations being worked on us, it would appear that the media are particularly suspect, if that is a strong enough word. For centuries the young have rebelled against authority. But can we suppose that the current levels of rebellion would be so high if it were not for the Saturday morning cartoons? Would the sexual revolution have gone so far without the ways that the media have made lechery commonplace? People may claim that the tube has no effect on them. But the claim sounds pathetic in the light of the sixty billion or so dollars that the advertisers are spending this year.

It would seem that the media use of indirect suggestion is the one we need most be aware of. The direct violence and sex are bad enough, and many will find ways to argue that these have negligible effect on conduct. However, when a serious person faces a temptation, whether he yields or not, he knows he faces a crisis. When he catches sight of something rotten, his guard goes up, whether he then watches it or not. Indirect suggestion is another matter. It comes under his guard in a relaxed setting. It might be established that the clever ads and innocent-seeming comedies teach more materialism and deaden more consciences than the blatant material.

If this matter intrigues you, try your own study of suggestion in the media, perhaps with attention to their use of subliminal techniques. All those uses may be ethically wrong, but your people are the constant victims, and you are their shepherd.

Honest Preaching

How then do we apply principles of suggestion in our preaching? By conveying those ideas and impressions that reinforce our message and by eliminating so far as possible those things that undercut it. If we believe in the importance of what we are doing, this sense of importance will show itself in dozens of ways, most of them unconscious. Indeed, honesty and urgency will cover a multitude of blunders and poor choices of words. More than that, doing our sermonic homework will convey the value we place on preaching, just as lack of preparation and lack of specifics will reveal the careless attitude that our people will sense. Compare the impact of these two statements: "Last week as I was praying about this sermon . . ." as against, "Last night as I was wondering what to preach about. . . ." Both statements may be honest, but the one is devastating.

Just as the wise minister used missionary illustrations to lay a foundation, we can through the judicious use of suggestion prepare our hearers for decisions they may not yet be ready to make. It does not take much pastoral experience to learn what can happen if we spring surprises in business meetings. On the other hand, if you want an addition to the building, you plant the idea first. You sound out your leaders individually and get them to pray with you. Put out hints discreetly; weigh the resistance. Give it time. Eventually the members begin to feel that it was their own idea, and you avoid all manner of lacerations. So much the better if you do not care who gets the credit for the idea.

Another great value to us is that we can become aware of what hints to keep out of our preaching. Ethnic references may be inoffensive to many of our hearers, but enough people are sensitive that we might as well keep our sermons clean of such distractions. On the other hand, if

How Does Suggestion Work?

you begin an illustration by saying, "A rabbi once told me—" you not only eliminate any suggestion of malice, but you convey that you're sympathetic to people outside the ivory tower some think we live in.

You may think of telling illustrations from suspect sources. You may well know of events in books or theatricals of which you disapprove. If you need the illustration, there has to be a way to give it without conveying that you approve of the medium. Why needlessly scar a sensitive conscience in some of those who hear you? Or why suggest a dangerous love for the world, when some of our people are already yearning for more of the world?

A bad word in amateur radio is "extraneous emissions," unintended vibrations that interfere with the neighbors' TV or stereo. We preachers spin off our own extraneous emissions: little hints of greed, materialism, profanity, gluttony or lust. These hints have a way of nullifying the message of the Cross and of a holy walk. It is not just that we need to be on guard against what might come out and to keep it masked. The real need is to keep short accounts with God and to pray for cleansing from secret faults. If we regard iniquity in our hearts, our people almost certainly will hear us, and soon they may be regarding the same iniquities in their hearts.

A pastor once suggested that his families come to church in separate cars, that the full parking lot would be good advertising for the church. The word out afterward was that some of his most faithful members wrote him off as insincere.

On the other hand, how many of us have made lifetime decisions on hearing some pastor or trusted friend remark,

"You've read *Pilgrim's Progress* by now."

"Isn't that just like the Lord?"

"I'm sure he felt he was doing the right thing."

"I wouldn't want to be doing any other kind of work."

In summary, whether we intend to or not, we are constantly putting out suggestions, many of them in the form of unconscious hints and body language. When we are leading others, we need to be alert to what ideas we are planting and how we are planting them. We need to be honest and right before God, like the man who was never caught off guard because he never needed to be on guard. If we are honest and right with God, we do not much need to worry about Freudian slips and body language, the suggestions we may be spinning off unawares. Even our errors will be on the side of the angels, and our sincere urgency will make it easy for love to cover our pulpit sins.

QUESTIONS FOR DISCUSSION

1. To what extent are these principles ways to manipulate people? To what extent are they legitimate tools of leadership?

2. For the spiritual ministry, what principles of suggestion are particularly important?

3. In sermons you have heard, in what ways have men negated their impacts by suggesting ideas contrary to what they were trying to get across?

4. How do the mechanics of delivery bear on this whole subject?

5. How appropriate is your church's advertising? How Biblical is it?

6. How does this whole subject bear on pulpit fire?

CHAPTER 14
CLEAR PHRASING

Style, choice of words, phrasing—why should they be so important? When we have learned by example that approximations are close enough, should we go to all the work to find the precise word? When our schools rarely demanded precise English of us, were not their values right? Does not evangelistic fervor go with a certain crudity of expression? Is it quite spiritual to put time and effort into learning the mother tongue with precision?

Probably we can agree that all these are merely ways by which some may rationalize their laziness. How many of our schools make clear, correct English a requirement for graduation? How many teachers are playing the game by passing along pupils who cannot spell, punctuate or put a clear sentence together? The post-baby-boom crisis in enrollment can hardly help the situation, when almost all schools are under pressure to admit students. Whatever the problems we may have to live with in all our ministries, can we agree that lucid and correct English does help us get the gospel out? And that it is no shame to work at speaking and writing lucid English?

We may sometimes think with images, but we communicate with words. How much of clear thinking is the precise use of words? When the gospel of grace is in no way what the natural mind would expect it to be, if we want to get that gospel across, we must choose our words with care. We can hardly hope that some divine alchemy will transform our obscurities into precisions in the minds of our people. A copy rarely improves on its original, and we can hardly expect a church member to have clearer concepts than his preacher has. How many of us have led an unusually vital service or class, and then given our hearers a quiz on what we thought had been wonderfully clear, only to have been astonished at how little we must have gotten into their minds? We have more or less constant losses in communication, and we are under constant obligation to cut those losses as much as possible, to make our messages as clear as we possibly can. This means that we must drive ourselves to prepare, to write and to speak with all the clarity we can achieve.

While composition in general is important, this chapter is going to

Clear Phrasing

concentrate on phrasing the points in our outlines. We may hope that whatever gains we make here will have far-reaching effects all through our communicating. In any case, we have to phrase our propositions and outline heads clearly, or we stand to have serious losses in comprehension among those who sit there.

Is It Spiritually Important?

This concern has come up before in this book. On the one hand it is possible to make almost any passage of the Bible sound like a cliché, and on the other hand, some preachers can make that same passage sound like water out of the rock. A criterion we need to insist on is that every vital component of a sermon ought to carry a certain urgency, a tang of reality. Some phrasings have this. We have to believe that all the Bible is important; but only some phrasings convey that importance.

For the proposition this spiritual importance is partly a matter of phrasing and partly a matter of where you are going with it. One approach we can rule out is "Every one of us should realize the truth of this passage." As you notice, it rarely turns out to be the decision we really want; look longer at the truth we should realize. What's more, this proposition will fit any chapter in the Bible. It comes in the same class as "We should live for God."

But for many preachers even this would be an advance over their current habit of preaching without a proposition. How many congregations will hear this week that there are three things in this passage? Perhaps,

I. The Past Blessings
II. The Present Blessings
III. The Permanent Blessings

Or the three *be*'s of the good church member

I. Be Present
II. Be Interested
III. Be Generous

These trivial phrasings come from a failure to preach for decision, and they suggest a mind that is soon bored with Bible study. If you have a proposition that asks for a specific decision, it will probably strike the people as important. Therefore it is at least a beginning to preach that we should live for God. It is an advance to preach that we should have a forgiving spirit. But this, too, limps. Preach that we should forgive those who hurt us, and the auditorium may get suddenly quiet.

Spiritual importance also shows in the main heads. Who has not heard the four looks that some preachers have found somewhere?

I. The Inward Look
II. The Backward Look
III. The Upward Look
IV. The Outward Look

With a little ingenuity they might have found three more, equally barren. Or some might have rephrased their divisions into something like these:

We must fix our minds on Christ. How? The writer here gives us several steps by which we may fix our minds on Him:

I. By Admitting Our Bent to Sin
II. By Remembering God's Past Benefits
III. By Praying Directly to Him
IV. By Concerning Ourselves with Others

Clear, specific, Biblical statements tend to have the ring of spiritual importance about them. The more general a statement, the more it sounds like something we have heard before.

Again, certain words convey power because they touch sensitive nerves. Not long ago a conference speaker delivered a rather routine message to a college group. As he began to apply the sermon, he dropped the word "virginity" almost as quietly as an arrow leaves a bowstring. The impact was like an arrow piercing the heart. The hall became instantly quiet as he elaborated his remark. He seemed to have nearly total attention for the rest of his sermon.

Is it spiritually important?

A second criterion seems to contradict the first:

Is It Simple?

The principle of economy is that we use as few words and syllables as we need. Two standard writers who have made this point are Rudolph Flesch and William Strunk. Their point is that while we need a few filler words to sound human, we are clearest when we use short words and

Clear Phrasing

short sentences. We would all probably agree that the best pulpit scholarship does not sound pedantic; it clothes itself in simplicity and practicality. The wise preacher keeps his points under control, long enough to say what he means, but still brief. Before he has finished writing out a long proposition, he is already thinking of ways to shorten and clarify it. If he finds himself writing, "We ought to exemplify the transforming power of God in our behavior," his antenna is already turning. The statement is true, but who will grasp it? It cries out to be shortened.

Examples abound. For us who preach, a look through our files will probably turn up one of two extremes, either something like

I. Sovereign Care
II. Saving Care
III. Sanctifying Care

An early section of the chapter disposed of these. Or we find the opposite impulse: I. By Living Our Lives in Such a Way as to. . . . It is not done yet, and it is already running into too many words. Or try these, which are at least more specific than the "Cares" above:

I. By Demonstrating Unity of Mind
II. By Exhibiting a Loving Attitude
III. By Possessing a Forgiving Spirit

Note that all these are cluttered, and a first step would be to revise the purr-words "Demonstrating," "Exhibiting" and "Possessing." Then it would look like this:

I. By Showing Unity of Mind
II. By Showing a Loving Attitude
III. By Having a Forgiving Spirit

But on second thought, the three words we have changed are only filler-words, and these verbs have little to do with the point of each statement. What we probably meant was something like

I. By Thinking Alike
II. By Loving One Another
III. By Forgiving Quickly

Compare these with the first attempt to get rid of the purr-words, and notice how brevity goes with clarity and force.

Brevity may not be an absolute, but any long proposition or main head is guilty until we can prove it innocent. It is worth the work either to justify or to change every last word until we get exactly what we need.

Is it simple?

Is It Exact?

He was preaching on the nature of Biblical love, with a textual sermon on 1 Corinthians 13:7. His proposition was that we should love one another, and his four main heads could hardly be faulted:

I. By Bearing All Things
II. By Believing All Things
III. By Hoping All Things
IV. By Enduring All Things

As he preached, his first head elaborated the patience that true love will show. As he launched into his second head, we were expecting something on the way that love trusts the beloved, and on the way that love wants to believe the best, even if the other person has spoken what seemed like an unkind word. But instead of what looked so obvious, the preacher began discussing the believer's credit rating and the need for keeping current on one's bills.

See if you can see any clear connection between his discussion and "Love believeth all things."

A student preacher was dealing with the theme, "God hates sin." His text was Romans 12:21, on not being overcome with evil. To try to find a logical connection between his theme and the verse is difficult, even if the two ideas are tangent to each other. It looked as if he had missed the context altogether. He seemed not to have exegeted the verse. He should have found another text that exactly conveyed his burden.

A main head needs to be short and clear. It also needs to state as precisely as possible the intent of the Biblical writer. This caution becomes even more urgent if the heads seem to alliterate. As this book has shown in a previous chapter, alliteration tempts a preacher to make a passage say what he needs it to say to make the alliteration come out right, and this is a danger to honest precision. We should caution ourselves against phrasing a point so as to make it fit some plan, whether it be to fit our word pattern, our church distinctives or our theology.

Clear Phrasing

Try this one: The sermon was on Joel 3:13, whose context deals with the final judgment of the Gentile forces in the Day of the Lord. The verse says, "Put ye in the sickle, for the harvest is ripe: come, get you down; for the press is full, the fats overflow; for their wickedness is great." The sermon, however, had to do with evangelism, and asked us to take up

    I. The Sickle of Preaching
    II. The Sickle of Prayer
    III. The Sickle of Persuasion

Except for the word "sickle," the preacher showed us no connection between his text passage and his sermon. Charity can forgive the tricky handling of the Word of God, but honest precision would have made it unnecessary to forgive.

It usually takes discipline to get the phrasing we need. Sometimes the outline seems to fall into our hands; the passage opens out in moments. Other passages seem to grin back and defy us to open them out. Here we must demand precision and clarity, whatever the time and energy these might require.

Is it exact?

Is It Strong?

How much force does it have? To repeat the specifics of strong phrasing, the key is the verb: an action verb rather than a state-of-being verb, in the active voice rather than in the passive, and in the affirmative, not in the negative. The person who writes with such verbs is likely to be clear. If only he keeps his sentence length under control and uses words with precision, his thinking is likely to be clear and compelling. The active voice requires a subject, and this removes any doubt as to who is doing the action. This would explain the way a bureaucrat takes cover behind the passive voice. However, the preacher has nothing to hide and everything to gain by the clearest, strongest phrasing. We should preach in the active voice.

Against the use of verbs, we often hear outlines that lean on nouns:

    I. The Content of Faith
    II. The Commitment of Faith
    III. The Compulsion of Faith

Sometimes we get adjectives:

I. By the Man of God Being Determined
II. By the Man of God Being Diligent
III. By the Man of God Being Loving
IV. By the Man of God Being Humble

Some do it with adverbs:

I. Because God Hears Us Constantly
II. Because God Hears Us Tenderly
III. Because God Hears Us Intelligently

As against all these weak patterns, the action verb or participle strikes the mind with force. It gives us a decision to make, a crisis to face. Instead of saying,

I. Because of Chastening

it says,

I. Because God May Chasten Us

The difference is profound: The first only hints at a reason; the second one states it.

Just as the words "Because of" are a symptom of weakness, a whole class of verbs ought to jog our minds. These are words like appreciate, realize, exemplify, demonstrate, manifest, recognize, elucidate—all high-sounding polysyllables, but words that in outlines do not mean much. Each one should carry a flashing red light. The moment we find ourselves writing such a word, we could well ask what we really mean. When they turn up in a proposition or main head, we should ask if a shorter, specific word would serve better. As when we find a passive voice, such words ought to pull us up short and press us to find a stronger way to say it. Those words are weak.

The same caution applies to nouns and adjectives. A brilliant professor used to urge us to establish this or that relationship. It sounded great in the classroom, but from the pulpit it doesn't much help our people. This applies to aspects, attitudes, conceptions, distinctions, impressions, parameters, phases, manifestations—all words that have right uses. But when we are tempted to use them in a proposition or main head, we should hold them the same way we do the long proposition:

133

Clear Phrasing

guilty until proved innocent. People do not need our learned complexities. They need the Bible in plain language.

Is it strong?

This chapter has to do with making good sermon outlines. Let us trust, however, that these principles make enough sense to apply in all our writing and preaching. Some sentences are more important than others, but all have a right to speak clearly and with force. It is worth the work to apply these cautions even while writing a friendly letter to the family, because these cautions have a great deal to do with communicating.

QUESTIONS FOR DISCUSSION

1. What reason do we have to believe that short words usually carry more meaning than long words?

That the active voice is stronger than the passive?

That an action verb is stronger than "to be"?

That a verb is stronger than a noun?

That short sentences are clearer than long ones?

2. Can we find any rules for gauging what is spiritually important? To what extent is it a matter of subjective judgment?

CHAPTER 15

THE TEXTUAL SERMON

It would be hard to find a verse to tell us how long a passage we should preach. For this book, at least, the preference is for a sizable passage of Scripture, hence the choice of expository preaching. For variety's sake, however, we will find occasions in which preaching one verse does something we could not otherwise do—stamp that verse on the minds of our people.

A textual sermon is not a topical sermon, even if they each begin with a single verse. You develop a topical sermon with your own insights and ideas. You develop a textual sermon by means of its own internal structure. For example, compare these three outlines on 1 Timothy 2:8: "I will therefore that men pray every where, lifting up holy hands, without wrath and doubting."

Proposition: We must pray fervently. How? Paul gives us in this verse several ways to pray fervently:

  I. By Using Any Place We Are
  II. By Offering Clean Hands to God
  III. By Clearing Our Minds

Or this approach, also textual

We must pray fervently. How? Paul in this verse gives us several steps of fervent prayer.

  I. By Judging Our Sins (no unconfessed sin)
  II. By Forgiving Our Debtors (no wrath)
  III. By Rejoicing Frankly (no negativism)

Now as against these, examine this:

We must pray fervently. Why? As we look at this principle, we may come up with several clear reasons why we must pray fervently.

  I. Because Prayer Enjoys Fellowship with God
  II. Because Prayer Is an Act of Faith
  III. Because Prayer Pleases God
  IV. Because Prayer Lays Hold of Divine Willingness

Actually, this last is not such a bad outline, but note that even if it is Biblical, you will not very well find those reasons in the verse. Most topical preaching would seem even more to rest on human inference or contrivance than on anything in the verse itself.

Advantages in Textual Preaching

Perhaps the supreme advantage of the textual sermon is the way that it concentrates on a small chunk of Scripture. If you want to stamp a particular verse on your people's memory, it will not be easy to do this in the course of a thirty-minute expository sermon. To preach your whole sermon on that single verse should of itself make the verse memorable. With any imagination and preparation you should accomplish your purpose.

A second advantage in the textual sermon is that it does preach the Bible; and rightly done, it does get that small chunk of Scripture across. A topical sermon may or may not get much Bible in. A sword-drill sermon may claim to be Biblical, but with its diffused effect it can hardly hope to leave even one passage impressed on the memories of the hearers. A running commentary may likewise claim to preach the Bible; but, as a previous chapter remarked, the impact of any one verse is unlikely to be deep.

A third advantage of a textual sermon is that it offers a certain simplicity that the expository sermon might have difficulty matching. An expositor has a lot to think of—content, skeleton, audience, delivery; and in the process it is not always easy to get the vitals across clearly. Neither is it easy to match the vitals of proposition and heads to the corresponding parts of the text passage and to get those things across. On the other hand, when you are preaching a single verse, it may take work to get the strongest possible phrasing of the proposition and heads, but from there on it should be easy to put it across simply and clearly.

Disadvantages in Textual Preaching

As against these advantages, textual preaching as a steady diet carries certain problems. For one, it does not get as much Bible across, although anyone could argue that a capable textual preacher is going to teach more Bible than a poor expositor. A more serious problem is how clearly a church will be able to see a whole book. A capable expositor might cover the book of Romans in about six weeks, using three services a week. In such a series he might be able to give a pretty clear picture of the total message of the book. With textual sermons you are looking at two or three years to cover Romans. For all that treatment you will find it a real challenge to give any clear overview of the book itself.

In his adult Sunday School class a certain preacher took more than six years to teach the book of Revelation. We may hope that his people got some gems along the way, because they seemed to get only the haziest idea of what the whole book is about. He gave them an abundance of details; but a twenty-four week series would probably have left them with more knowledge of the book. A pity.

Requirements for Textual Preaching

If expository preaching obligates us to exegete the passage, it would seem that textual preaching requires its own intensive study of the verse. The longer the passage that we preach, the less problem we have from any one imprecision in our exposition of it. If we are preaching a single verse and get something wrong, the whole message will suffer a greater distortion. To do it right, we should probably spend as much time studying this week's verse as we took for last week's chapter.

The textual approach then requires probably greater attention to the context. For example, note the difficulty in understanding Romans 15:1 if we have not already devoured 14:1–3. Or for an extreme case, try John 6:53 apart from the rest of the chapter. The textual approach requires a more intensive word study and at least as much attention to the sentence structure of the verse. On the other hand, the textual approach gives you more time for this verse-intensive study, as well as for consulting everything in your library that bears on it. For those of us who have covered our walls with commentaries, this is the moment of truth. For the man who owns all ten volumes of Kittel's *Theological Dictionary of the New Testament,* here is his chance to draw at length on all that accumulated wisdom.

Another requirement in textual preaching, at least as important as in any other approach, is meditation. When it seems that many sermonic dishes are served raw, the slow simmer of meditation offers a new quality, a new succulence, to what we serve. Many insights come only with time, but since those insights give freshness and vitality to a sermon, it is worth the time to wait for them to come. The chapter on imagination dealt with this at greater length.

The Textual Sermon

A third requirement in textual preaching is the analysis of the verse structure. What is the leading verb? What is the core idea? For an easy verse, consider 2 Chronicles 7:14. For one that is not so easy, try John 3:16 or Galatians 2:20. To get a regular, coherent outline from either of these will draw hard on your mental powers, and careful verse analysis will be the royal gateway to logical organization.

A fourth requirement, then, in textual preaching is good organization. This begins with the proposition; all the criteria still apply, and shortcuts lead to the bogs. Is it not enough to assume a proposition? Well, write it out and see what it looks like. Do you have to preach the proposition verbatim? If you do not, how many will get the idea? Probably not many. At this point the methodical approach leads to Biblical clarity. If a man wants to spin gossamer webs or play sermonic violin music, let him do it in the illustrations and explanations. The sermon vitals have to be cast-iron specifics. If you want your people to follow your thinking, by all means spell it out for them. State each main head distinctly, and do not be ashamed to repeat it for emphasis.

The principles governing the divisions still apply. The main heads should cover the verse and stay within it. They should be parallel in form and not overlap. Since they all cover the same verse, you can hardly worry about the undergirding, as in an expository outline. But the phrasing has to have force, and everything the chapter on phrasing said about this applies in the textual sermon. Again, the key to each main head is the verb in it: an action verb in the active voice, phrased in the affirmative.

As you finish your preparation, guard yourself against the impulse to make a sword drill out of it. It is perfectly in line with clarity to refer to other passages of Scripture, but if you have us turn to more than one or two, you lose us. If you just quote them or perhaps read them to us, you can hope that we will follow your message. If you ask us to turn to several, you can be assured that we will get lost somewhere along the winding path.

In choosing between textual and expository sermons, we have to keep asking how best to get the Word across. Expository outlines of themselves are little help if we do not point our people to specific verses and lines. We have to juggle about nine plates at a time: to make the Bible clear, to pursue our goal, to watch our people, to love them, to keep them interested, to keep our pitch down, to touch the conscience, to keep things clear and to quit on time.

138

A veteran missionary in a conference remarked that you can make an evangelist in about two weeks; to make a Bible teacher takes twenty years. Whatever the truth in his words, we may suppose that there is no quick way to make a Bible preacher.

Textual, Type II

There is another kind of textual sermon—let us call it Type II. For most of us, twice a year is quite enough to use it, but for variety it has value, and it should make a short verse unforgettable.

Pick a short verse, say, 1 Thessalonians 5:18, "In every thing give thanks: for this is the will of God in Christ Jesus concerning you." Now get a good illustration for the verse, perhaps the account of Jesus and the ten lepers. The sermon then proceeds like this:

You tell the story of the ten lepers. You then summarize it with the verse, "In every thing give thanks. . . ."

You give another illustration having to do with gratitude. You summarize it with the verse, "In every thing give thanks. . . ."

You give an explanation of what thanks actually involves. You show the kinship between the New Testament words for thanks, grace and favor. You then repeat the verse.

And so on for twenty-five or thirty minutes. It may not carry much profound exegesis, but it is a way to stamp a verse on the minds of your people by a sort of rhythmic repetition. It is like hammering a nail in. A series of strokes accomplishes your purpose. In this case, the simplicity and the limited purpose cut the need for an outline. Each illustration or explanation leads back to repeating the verse. Whatever else they may get out of the message, they will almost surely get one distinct passage of the Bible to carry away in their minds.

QUESTIONS FOR DISCUSSION

1. In what ways is textual preaching better than expository? In what ways is expository better?

2. Why was preaching in the early church mainly on longer passages, while since the Reformation most preaching seems to have been textual, or topical on a short text?

The Textual Sermon

3. Why do we not have Biblical examples to draw from?

4. When the great preachers of the last century preached single verses, is it not presumption to advocate a different pattern?

5. How important is structure to the textual sermon? To what extent is the outline just a handy frame to hang your ideas on?

CHAPTER 16

AUTHORITY IN YOUR PREACHING

"For though I should boast somewhat more of our authority, which the Lord hath given us for edification, and not for your destruction, I should not be ashamed" (2 Cor. 10:8).

"According to the [authority] which the Lord hath given me" (2 Cor. 13:10).

Authority is an elusive quality. From the point of view of the congregation, it varies with the hearer's respect for the preacher. From the point of view of the preacher, authority is whatever commands that respect. As a preacher you want that respect for the message you preach, but you have to merit respect for yourself as a person. If this seems too self-evident to need saying, consult your own memories. How often can you remember hearing a sermon that helped you, despite the fact that it came from the lips of a preacher you did not respect? How hard was it for you to dissociate your attitude toward the one from your attitude toward the other? To say this a bit differently, you need to carry authority as a person in order that your message might carry authority.

A Sense of Call

"There's many a slip 'twixt call and ship" (missionary maxim).

While this book treated the call in the first chapter, the matter fits here. Ever since Moses, Samuel, Isaiah, Jeremiah, Ezekiel, the Apostles and Paul, prophets of God have regarded themselves as called to service. No two of them had precisely the same experience, but all of them shared a conviction that God had in some way drafted them. Some, like Jeremiah, Ezekiel and Jonah, resisted that summons. Some, like Jeremiah and Peter, tried to get out of it later on. With Paul his ministry was no mere preference of his own. "Necessity is laid upon me; yea, woe is unto me, if I preach not the gospel! For if I do this thing willingly, I have a reward: but if against my will, a [stewardship] of the gospel is [entrusted to] me" (1 Cor. 9:16, 17).

Since a call to preach has a subjective element in it, various writers have questioned whether such a thing as a call even exists. They seem to regard the prophets and the apostles as exceptions. By this light pastors and missionaries have instead followed a worthy vocational preference. For all the verses these men use in defense of their view, I believe that the real force of Scripture is on the side of a personal call. There may be reason to debate the matter of a call. Is it possible to preach without one? Jeremiah 23:21 would say that it is possible: "I have not sent these prophets, yet they ran: I have not spoken to them, yet they prophesied." Is it possible to be called and not preach? Jonah would seem to be the example of this, but the Lord got him eventually. I suppose most of us can name men we love who once gave evidence or testimony of a call to the ministry but who for one reason or another have gone to other occupations. Some of these might affirm even yet their call.

Most of us who preach have some sense of a divine call. By whatever means it came, we have the conviction that God has given us this summons. We cannot resist it, or else we can resist it only at some peril or misery. No two of us seem to have the same testimony. Some of us doubtless have a stronger conviction than others. If, however, you have met God over the matter, you don't just believe—you *know* that God has called you. Whether your sermon is good or not, you preach with a divine mandate. This mandate may not assure a good sermon, but it puts you under a terrible obligation to preach a good one.

Probably most of us would agree that we do not preach new revelations or additions to Scripture. The call does not of itself apply to content; it has to do with the speaker. Of itself it does not assure the power of the Holy Spirit (alas!), but it obligates us to seek God for that power. It does not seem to assure the fruit of the Spirit. Our own experience will bear out that Jonah was not the last one who, despite his call, was able to preach without love or much joy or peace or longsuffering.

Our right comes down to this: "I do not have a choice. God called me to preach, and woe is me if I quit." Whatever there is to preaching with authority, at least some of it comes from the sense of personal mandate. You can stand at the pulpit because you know that God has in some way willed that you stand there.

Scripture: The Source and the Content of the Message

The second basis for our authority as preachers is the source of what we preach. Paul told Timothy to preach the Word. This book presupposes that the Bible is the verbally inspired, inerrant Word of God and that it is uniquely profitable for doctrine, reproof, correction and instruction in righteousness. We may or may not be able to impress people with our own opinions or values. If we can impress them with these things, we succeed as entertainers or moralists. As prophets we succeed only to the extent that we preach Scripture. The call of God accredits our presence. The Word of God accredits our message. To preach with authority we need both.

How does the Bible give a preacher such authority and confidence in the pulpit? First of all because the Bible is absolute truth (Ps. 119:89, 160). As absolute truth it remains constant despite our shifting understanding. We preach a fixed and infinite value, and to the extent that we preach Scripture, our preaching conveys the authority of Scripture.

"Don't Take My Word for It"

I recently heard the testimony of a man who tried to lead his tough old crony to the Lord. His approach was simple. He put his Bible in front of his friend, opened to the evangelistic passage and asked him to read it. He then asked what the passage meant. By his later testimony, his friend needed no explanations or persuasions; the Bible did its own work.

A certain pastor seemed unusually successful in bringing his children to follow the Lord. When someone asked him and his wife how they were doing it, they answered that while the story was far from over yet, they tried to put all their discipline in terms of Scripture. In any confrontation they tried to remember to ask, "What does the Bible tell you to do right now?" or, "What does God's Word say?"

As we preach the Bible, we have the same position of strength.

But what if someone answers that the Biblical absolute loses authority as it passes through our minds and lips? We need to face the truth of this. Almost anything we say from the pulpit we tend to modify in the direction of our own interests and traditions. Any librarian can comment on how quickly science books go out of date, and in less than a decade; and human experiment keeps correcting them. In somewhat the same way our theology books and commentaries tend to go out of date in less than a century, and new Biblical insight keeps correcting these. Similarly, our opinions and values may follow Scripture; but the more we study Scripture, and prayerfully make it our own, the more it will correct our ideas. Even though our sermons may only approximate Scripture, as we faithfully study the Word, we can hope for an ever-increasing fidelity to the Word. In this way we can heighten the authority with which we preach it.

The Power of the Word

Not only is the Bible true. It is also quick and powerful (Heb. 4:12). No other book can approach that claim. This verse is in fact saying that God's Word is inherently living and powerful, that apart from such other energy as God may bring to bear, there is something about the Bible that carries its own power, all by itself. It distinguishes between soul and spirit as a sword might cut between the joint and the marrow. It discerns the thoughts and intents of the heart, which is to say that the Word itself has the power to criticize, to pass judgment on, a person's innermost musings and intentions.

The Need for the Word

The Bible gives us authority to preach, not only because it is true, not only because it carries its own power, but also because man needs it. Moses wrote and Jesus said that man shall not live by bread alone, but by every word coming from the mouth of God. Yet the human mind has ever since been trying to find ways to ignore this principle. Many of our people believe that daily Bible reading is a desirable option, but only that. They seem to accept the notion that ultimate truth can come by watching the eleven o'clock news, by reading the *Reader's Digest* and by looking at flowers.

The notion contains an element of truth. Both Psalm 19 and Romans 1 agree that a man can learn enough from nature and by natural wisdom to make him eternally accountable before God. The natural, fallen mind can know God's power and deity, leaving man without excuse (Rom. 1:20). He can also get a pretty good idea of what constitutes sin (Rom. 2). But think of all that man cannot grasp by himself. Only by the Bible can he find out about the Trinity. Only by the Bible can he know the nature of the Incarnation, of God revealing Himself through His Son. Only by the Bible can he find out about God's love. Only by the Bible can he know the meaning of the Cross or the plan of salvation. How many rabbis ever discovered that Messiah must suffer? How many Old Testament saints ever saw Messiah in the levitical sacrifices? Jesus expressed surprise that Nicodemus did not understand the new birth, but can we not sympathize with Nicodemus?

Some of our people are convinced that they can live all right without daily Bible study. But apart from a Biblical understanding, nature's God is a cruel God. Cats eat sparrows, lions eat gazelles and fish eat other fish. Widows are bereaved, the rich prosper and the righteous suffer. Without a Biblical understanding, the universe runs by Murphy's Law, and the shrewd observer easily lives below Schaeffer's "line of despair." Then the universe has neither a rational nor a moral basis of existence.

The Bible then is the necessary Book, and as we preach it, it enables us to preach with authority. Indeed, it requires us to preach. When a man hears that a tornado has been sighted nearby, he has a duty to spread the warning. His message authorizes him to shout above the talk or music that others may be listening to. Even so our message; the Bible authorizes us to preach, as it were, to break in on the thoughts of others.

Experience

A further basis for preaching with authority is our experience of the validity of our message. How much easier for a salesman to sell a product he has used and liked rather than something he has personally never tried. Even the unsaved public expects a preacher to be real.

There are limits to the experiences we need to have. We can promise victory over liquor, even if we have never actually wrestled with whiskey ourselves. We can offer freedom from drugs, even if we ourselves have never taken more than two aspirins at a time. We are not phonies, provided we have known the saving grace of Christ, provided we have personal acquaintance with Christians who once were enslaved to liquor or drugs and provided we have had some parallel victories over sins and habits.

There is an account about the late Dr. Harry Ironside, who was once preaching in a street meeting. During his sermon someone passed him a note. He glanced at it and read it to the crowd. It was an invitation to debate Christianity versus agnosticism, at a nearby hall at four that afternoon. He accepted the challenge on two conditions: first, that the writer of the note produce that afternoon an ex-alcoholic, who had gone to the depths and lost everything to drink, but a person who had now come to light through the principles of agnosticism and who was now living a respectable life before the community free from the temptation to drink because of his newfound faith. Second, the challenger must produce a woman now walking in radiant victory. She must be a woman who was once debauched in a life of prostitution, a woman who had found new life through the principles of agnosticism and was now a credit to the community. Ironside went on to say he believed that he could assemble perhaps a hundred such persons by the hour of four that afternoon, persons whose lives Christ had transformed through personal faith in Him. According to the account, a voice came from the crowd to say that there was no use debating on Ironside's terms, that he had never heard of agnosticism changing a life in that way and that he was withdrawing his challenge.

Jesus could say to the crowd, "Which of you convinceth me of sin?" (John 8:46). Whatever our sins and frailties, there is such a thing as a cleansed conscience. Peter could preach with confidence and authority in Acts 3:13 and 14: "Whom ye delivered up. . . . But ye denied the Holy One and the Just." He could use that language because he had such a complete sense of the forgiveness of his own denial. As we have experience with God in confession and claiming forgiveness, we can preach with the same confidence and authority.

Preparation

A fourth basis for preaching with authority is our preparation. If God has called us, if we are preaching Scripture and if our experience accredits our sermon, so far so good. Even if we are forced to preach at a moment's notice, we preach with authority. If, however, we have time to prepare but fail to prepare adequately, some of that authority drains away.

While the truth of Scripture is an absolute, our use of that truth turns on how well we do our homework. If we prepare carelessly, our people will sense it, and so will we—and we will lose some of our fire. On the other hand, if we have done careful exegesis of the passage, this too will show itself in a number of ways. It will show in the precision of our explanations and in the richness of our understanding. It will show in our confidence and zest. It enhances our authority objectively by giving us more passion to preach.

Careful preparation gives us more than just the Biblical content; it gives fresh insights into the passage. The chapter on imagination deals with the values of the insights that come through reflection. These values

146

also bear on the authority with which we preach. If we have meditated on the passage and on our outline, we will have seen more than what a mere glance would see. Just as more exegesis means more expertise, so the more insights we gain, the more freshness and vitality we have. If we know that the sermon is fresh and unique, we can preach it with the more confidence. This confidence adds up to increased authority, which is to say, increased respect from our hearers.

Finally, preparation involves meeting God over our sermon. If we know that we have prayed for the message, that we have prayed in the process of organizing it and that we have prayed for the power of the Holy Spirit, we have reason to believe that God will hear and answer. With such spiritual preparation can we not trust that as we preach, we do represent God before men? Moses prayed, "Except thy presence go with us, lead us not up hence." Jacob prayed, "I will not let thee go except thou bless me."

As against such possibilities of speaking for God, how poor and tawdry if we descend to being mere performers. But are some getting away with so much less? May we never join their number. But is not entertainment building large churches? Not according to Scripture. But are all of us disposed to walk such a hard path when easier ways are at hand?

The prophets walked a hard path and accepted the loneliness of a walk with God.

QUESTIONS FOR DISCUSSION

1. To what extent can we share the authority with which Jesus taught (Matt. 7:29)?

2. This chapter has spoken of both authority and confidence. How do they relate to each other?

3. What characteristic words expressed the authority of the prophets? The authority of Jesus?

4. What connection do authority and passion have?

CHAPTER 17

WRAPPING IT UP— AND ON TIME

"Therefore let all the house of Israel know assuredly, that God hath made that same Jesus, whom ye have crucified, both Lord and Christ" (Acts 2:36).

There comes a time when you have said enough. Either you have finished preaching your main heads, or you are approaching the thirty-minute point. Whatever comes first, consider that you have said enough. It is time to tie things together. If you have left some questions unanswered, answer them now. If you have left threads hanging, tie them now. If you have been building suspense, resolve it now. It is time to stop, or better, to preach the conclusion that you had prepared.

You probably have your own tastes as to how to keep track of the time, but a few cautions apply. First, a clock on the wall invites people to watch it. If anyone is to do any clock-watching during your sermon, you want it to be yourself, not someone in your congregation. This argues for placing your own watch above your Bible, or even to have a clock set into the pulpit, like Spurgeon's. Haldeman's pulpit had a place inset to hold a large pocket watch. In neither man's case was there any danger of his timepiece falling off. Second, you want to keep eye contact, hence the advantage of not consulting a watch on your wrist. This would plant ideas that you do not want to plant. If you need to consult your watch, better if it is already in a secure place on your pulpit, where you and only you can see it. This requires breaking eye contact for only the shortest moment.

Should you introduce new material in your conclusion? Generally not. To move to other ground at this point is rhetorically jarring; save it for another sermon. With that said, there may be some developments that still fit the sermon. You might with consistency shift the mood so that after a serious, even somber message, you bring out the sunshine; or conversely, after a bright message your conclusion might take on a serious mood.

It is also possible that the solution to a passage may lie outside the

149

passage. If you have spent the whole sermon preaching against a given sin, to conclude with confession and repentance might seem to introduce new material. Your own wisdom should be able to sort this out so that to resolve tensions caused earlier in your sermon need not cause dissonance. It is one thing to drive through miles of country to reach a place in the city. It is something else on approaching the city to change your mind and to go to some different destination altogether.

Press the Conscience

An important truism holds that when you are pressing God's claims on people, their conscience is on your side. From the beginning of your message you have been preaching for a decision. Now is your time to appeal for that decision. You do well to plan the appeal you want to use. If your interrogative was "Why?" your heads were probably a series of reasons. Now is the time to weigh whether reason is indeed the motivation to which you are going to appeal. Reason, fear and self-interest are surely three common appeals we often give to the lost as we present to them the plan of salvation. And these are surely more appropriate than greed or pleasure or group approval.

Some respond from duty. Why do men toil all day in a mine or a mill? Many of them have families to support, and whatever the darkness or the drudgery, the job has to be done; it is their duty to do it. What makes men go off to war? Doubtless, all sorts of motives. What makes them stay at a post against impossible odds? Mostly the conviction that it has to be done. During the year-long battle of Verdun, what had been the town of Fleury changed hands sixteen times. A frontline machine gunner had a life expectancy of perhaps ten minutes. Countless men fought; nearly a million died, held at impossible posts by various motives, mostly duty.

Some respond from love. In a generation when the love of many has grown cold, you may question the idea of preaching that people should obey because they love the Lord. Nevertheless John 14:15 puts obedience with love, and it is surely Biblical to preach for both. Most of us could probably do more to encourage people to love the Lord Whom they sing about so glibly.

The other side of love is altruism, which is purposing the good of others. If we see little evidence of feeling for others, we can still preach to generate it or to rekindle any sparks of it as may lie in our people's

150

hearts. Why not preach to a man to receive Christ if only for the sake of the wife and children he loves? It may be spiritually suspect to pray for their happiness, but to preach for it would seem to be a legitimate appeal.

Some respond from aspiration, the selfless yearning to excel. As against ambition, which is a selfish determination to climb, aspiration is a willingness to burn out to reach a goal. Paul aspired to preach the gospel where it was unknown (2 Cor. 10). Couples have been known to aspire to reach the toughest mission field. Some preachers aspire to win numbers and to disciple them. Chapel sermons may not appeal to this as much as they used to, but there may still be young people who aspire to leave a mark on their generation. Three verses that use the word (but render it "labor" or "study") are Romans 15:20; 2 Corinthians 5:9; and 1 Thessalonians 4:11. Aspiration is Biblical.

Some respond from gratitude. Gratitude may be in short supply, and a mark of natural men is that they are unthankful (Rom. 1:21). Still there have to be traces of thanks that we can kindle into flame. If we want to see gratitude, we should preach for it, and gratitude can motivate people. Here we need to be careful. If we think that our people will be grateful to us for our selfless and Christlike service to them, we should think again. If we get them obligated to us, they will tend to resent the obligation and back away; if we want friends, it is better to find ways to obligate ourselves to them. But in any case, if we can encourage them to thank God deeply for all His benefits, we may generate a high motivation to which we can appeal.

Then there are some neutral motivations to which we may rightly appeal. That is, they involve no great virtue, but they may still Scripturally motivate people to right decisions. Fear of God is so often commended in Scripture that it may well belong to the class of high motivations. Fear of Hell is not so noble a thing, but it has driven countless lost men into the everlasting arms. Sheer self-interest is in the same class; it is a stupid prodigal who throws his life away in selfish desires, when he can find food and peace only in the house of his Father. Yet the Lord does not condemn the prodigal when self-interest is the only motivation that the Bible credits him with. On that basis we may reach lost people when we can think of no higher appeal to offer them. In the same class is satisfaction. When you get to the end of your present path, what satisfaction will you have when you look back? Will a life of creature comforts mean anything when you compare it with the satisfaction you could have in the service of the King of Kings? Compared with the Lord's work, what satisfaction can there be in merely keeping entertained so as to stave off boredom?

Also in the neutral class is the appeal to guilt, one of the most common appeals we find in use. We can put our people on a guilt trip for their failure to read their Bibles, to give, to win souls or to turn up for Thursday night visitation. On the other hand, if we focus on their guilt as offense against the infinitely Holy One, against Majesty we can barely conceive, we may awaken their conscience to the point of opening their hearts to Him. Of all the things that go wrong with the human soul, guilt is one for which we have a perfect and effectual cure.

While we are on the subject of motivations, can we rule out the low ones? There are ways to seek religious commitments by appealing to pride or greed, but why negate the message of the Cross by our appeal? Have we not all heard such words as, "Come on, gang, accept Christ and you will have more fun than you ever had before"? To offer pleasure is tempting. Who wants to come out to hear a prophet if he could hear a showman or a celebrity? How many will attend Bible teaching, in comparison with the number we can induce to attend a film, a musical presentation, gospel magic, puppet shows or chalk drawings? Some of these may be Biblically legitimate, but we do well to ask ourselves to what extent we may be using these as motivations and to what extent a given appeal may be spiritually defensible. We might find a great amount of pastoral experience to show the griefs of those who built works on those appeals; and then they realized how hard it is to build spiritual works using those who have been attracted by carnal appeals.

Clarify the Decision

How many of us have sat through invitations, willing to respond, but wondering whether we were supposed to or not?

Near the beginning of our sermon preparation we had a burden and a passage. Later on we formed a statement of purpose and a proposition to fit it. Ever since then we have made a series of holy calculations to make the Scriptural demands as clear and compelling as possible. Now we prepare to draw the net. What does it take to make it clear? A kind of explanation? An illustration? And having made it clear, with what words will we press for that decision? How confidently do we expect decisions?

Include an Evangelistic Appeal

What about an evangelistic appeal at the end of a sermon that was addressed to Christians? In reasonable consistency with what this chapter has said, it should be possible. Two generations ago lost people attended church if only because it was someplace to go, and often the Sunday evening service was frankly evangelistic. Thanks largely to the media, we no longer have this opportunity; but unsaved people do attend our services, and some of them know that they are unsaved. Is it possible to give them the gospel and still feed the flock that is among us? One solution is to preach nothing but salvation, and that sort of ministry makes so few spiritual demands on the believers that deacons have been known to insist on evangelistic preaching in every service.

On the other hand, it should be possible to preach the spiritual walk and still fulfill two evangelistic goals. First, include somewhere the plan of salvation. If the saints need more than this, they need at least this. It reminds them of the means by which God saved them and of the message that they need to give to their friends. Second, include an evangelistic appeal. It might go somewhat like this:

> Now, friends, this morning I have been preaching to Christians. But it may well be that some of you realize that this message is not for you, that what you need is to be saved. Frankly, you do not know where you are going to go when you die, but you would like to know. It may be that no one has ever gone over this with you. In a moment we are going to have prayer. After that, we are going to give you the opportunity to go into a quiet place where someone can show you what the Bible says about the destiny of your soul.

There was a story, perhaps factual, of a two-part series that D. L. Moody prepared to preach on successive Sunday nights. The year was 1871. The first sermon was on why we must be saved, and the second sermon was on how; and he deferred his gospel invitation to the second sermon. Between the two Sundays Chicago had its great fire, and three and a half square miles of Chicago lay in smoking ashes. In the disruption Moody lost all opportunity to draw the net he had placed. He then resolved that that would not happen again, that every time he preached, he would give sinners an appeal to receive Christ.

Quit While You Are Ahead

Of the rights we tend to claim as Heaven's ambassadors, one is our right to preach as long as we please. We might say it a bit more elegantly. We may preach as long as the Holy Spirit leads us to or as long as we need in order to cover the material or as long as we need so as to impress sacred truth on the hearts of our people. Great preachers of former generations preached a full hour or more, and why should we not preach that long if we please? After all, sermonettes make Christianettes.

T. T. Shields once wrote to V. I. Masters regarding Masters' forthcoming Sunday at Jarvis Street Baptist Church. In his letter, Shields asked that the sermons go not less than an hour. That was what his people were used to, and he did not want them spoiled. In May 1981, the late Ralph Chaliss, French Bible teacher, preached in a crowded gymnasium in Montreal. He held rapt attention from 7:50 to 9:50 P.M., exactly two hours. On the other hand most of us have sat through messages in which the preacher could have closed after twelve minutes; his people had simply quit listening.

How long should we preach? We do well to conclude in thirty minutes. For every one of us who can grip attention for much longer than that, there are eleven who by preaching too long are damaging their ministries and their churches. Most of those eleven are preaching to no-growth or negative-growth churches, and they may wonder why their numbers tend to shrink. For any reader who may find himself in this situation, he would do well to conclude in thirty minutes. If that seems arbitrary, then he could try for even less than that. Why?

A first reason to limit our length is the beatitude that says, "Blessed are the merciful." If we love our people, we will consider their limitations. The media have conditioned them to a short attention span, and most of us are simply not entertaining enough to meet that competition. We work for clear understanding when we limit our messages to half an hour or less, because that is about all the material that they are going to carry away anyway. And they will honestly appreciate the kindness.

Good pastors have disregarded this and injured their ministries. They have listened to urgent pleas for shorter messages and ignored those pleas. They may wonder why they had to move to other churches. If this seems like a selfish reason to keep under thirty minutes, then go back to the principle of mercy or go to the next paragraph.

A second reason to stay within thirty minutes is that the discipline works for clarity in our organization. We cut out the digressions and repetitions. Our words take on a certain urgency.

Our only loss is the leisure to say whatever we have the impulse to say. Since that impulse is easily a form of self-indulgence and not necessarily of the Spirit, it is a loss we can well afford.

Biblical writers worked within disciplines. The acrostic Psalms are examples, especially Psalm 119. Lamentations follows a similar limitation, at least through the first four chapters. John set limits in writing his Gospel, and clearly he left out all that did not fit his purpose. If this is also true of Luke's Gospel, it shows even more in the book of Acts. Here a careful study should make it plain that Luke used only what fit his purpose. When we work within a reasonable time span, the limitation should improve our thinking and increase our determination to tell God's truth with Holy Spirit power.

A third reason to quit on time is that enough is enough. There comes a time when we have said it, and to go on talking can only deaden the impact we have made. If we cannot make an idea clear and urgent in thirty minutes, ten or fifteen more minutes are not likely to help. We could have quit when we were not so far behind. A symptom of trouble is the promise, "Now in closing," or worse, "But we must hurry on." Either statement is liable to close some of the Bibles and most of the minds. Yet we can all remember hearing such promises that began another ten or fifteen minutes of verbiage. If you feel that you must promise a conclusion, it is better just to conclude, even with an abrupt ending, which may be better than just tailing off.

How do you stop? If your planned conclusion is not working, just stop. If you have not gone past thirty minutes, you will face a wave of gratitude. After more than thirty, you will probably get only resignation. Better to get thanks.

QUESTIONS FOR DISCUSSION

1. If the sermon conclusion involves a shift in mood or application, what principles ought to govern that shift?

2. Why is it important to preach for decision? In what ways does the conclusion figure in that purpose?

Wrapping It Up

3. How are motives important to God? Why is it vital for us to evaluate different motives and to know which ones we want to appeal to?

4. Just how important is it to stay within thirty minutes?

5. What does a well-prepared conclusion have to do with pulpit passion?

A LAST WORD

Our point in history calls for a fresh proclamation of the gospel of grace. We still take to our own hearts Paul's command to Timothy, "Preach the word; be instant in season, out of season; reprove, rebuke, exhort with all longsuffering and doctrine" (2 Tim. 4:2). We take it personally that we must proclaim the Word when we have a good opportunity as well as when we have to make our own opportunity. Paul's phrasing leaves us without excuse. Whether we have opportunity or not, we are to stand there ready and still find ways and occasions to preach the message. We are to bring people under conviction, to rebuke their sins and to encourage them, all the while being slow to steam up, and at the same time carrying on an educational program. Because, Paul warns us, the time will come when they will not put up with wholesome doctrine.

We face some definite challenges.

First, we hear repeated statements that preaching is no longer a valid means of communication. Under the jargon word "innovative," the avant-garde churches have tried films, dramas, panel discussions, book reports, role playing, dances, group therapy and almost any kind of platform discourse that avoids "The heart-burdened tones of the messenger of the Cross." Virtually our whole population has now been brought up on television, meaning we are used to an intimate medium, and our attention span is now millimeters long. The rest of the world is with us. Europe, including Russia, has about one television set for every three persons. Japan has one for four, and South America has about one for five. In the face of the profound social changes that have taken place in a generation, may we not wonder if preaching is still a viable means of Christian service. If, however, the Bible is still true, we have to believe that God still endorses preaching and that He still can use it.

A second challenge is the shift in the size of the local church. At this writing, the average size of a church is about seventy, which sets the little ones in the same calculation as the superchurches. It has been predicted that the big ones will survive and that most of the little ones will go under. In view of such a projection, might we wonder what future there is for the Bible expositor, when show business is the "proved" means of attracting new people?

A Last Word

A third great challenge is the cultural conditioning that the Western world has been subjected to. For this whole century we have been so bombarded with the humanist party line that even the elect seem about to believe it themselves. Three generations have been told that they got here by an evolutionary process. They have been told that there are no fixed values in the universe, no norms, no absolutes. The positivists have so taken over the social sciences that the believer finds himself on the defensive. Francis Schaeffer was doubtless right when he put the date at about 1910 when Western culture passed a line of despair; people despaired of any rational basis for existence and of any moral basis for existence. With no God left, there could be no more meaning in the universe. The implication for us is that preaching is like broadcasting radio programs to people who do not have radios. Most people are simply not equipped to pick up our language and concepts.

In the popular mind, preaching has divorced itself from reality. Two generations ago what was said from the pulpit was news, and the *New York Times* on Mondays would run perhaps a dozen accounts of what had been preached in major churches in the city. No longer. Now when someone comes out of church with a fresh idea, he might feel that he should register surprise if he were to tell someone what he received. We no longer respect preachers or their preaching as people did a century ago.

With that sort of conditioning, Bible Christianity has become an object of condescension at best or scorn at worst. It is the only religion that the media are permitted to treat with contempt, just as the American South is the only cultural entity that the media can publicly ridicule. Western culture has become increasingly materialistic, and the message of the Cross has thus become less and less relevant to current life. At the same time the saints have become increasingly materialistic, and the things of the Spirit of God have taken on an aura of unreality. Christian parents appear to be more concerned for their children's incomes than for their virtue, as any Bible college recruiter can abundantly testify. When Bible-believing church members seem less and less receptive to the things of the Spirit, will not preaching make us feel as though we were driving in low gear through sand?

With the challenges already mentioned, we seem to see a fourth: a heavy loss of our young people. While we rejoice at the ones who still show a sacrificial love for Christ, we wonder at the decline in their numbers during the last generation. Even the survivors seem changed. The old revulsion for the world seems to have lost its intensity. The willingness to sacrifice has diminished. The world's music and its lyrics have conditioned young people to a tolerance of sin, and the performers have become role models for the deacons' children.

George Peters once remarked in class about the verse that says the night cometh when no man can work. Not that no man will want to work; the Lord seemed to say that the time is coming when work will somehow no longer be possible. As we contemplate the times, we may gain fresh understanding of what the Lord meant.

Against these challenges, we still have the divine mandate to preach the Word. If preaching seems foolish, Paul anticipated that thought in 1 Corinthians 1:21–27 when he said that God is delighted to use the foolishness of that means to save the lost. We have to believe in the power of God to use His words on our lips to touch hearts. He still has the power to break down strongholds and lead every thought into captivity to Christ, and despite all the visual evidence to the contrary, we have His Word on which to base our confidence.

Elijah felt himself to be terribly alone, yet God told him that He had seven thousand heads of families who had not bowed the knee to Baal. We can preach with confidence that God still has His own out there and that they are to some degree hungry for the messages we are ready to preach to them. We have to believe that God still has His number out there—some who already love the Word and others who can by the power of the Spirit be brought to love it. Thus we can share Elijah's situation.

God has in recent history revealed that power. After the restoration of the British monarchy in 1660 and the Halfway Covenant in New England in 1661, the English-speaking world went into spiritual decline for most of a century. Then in the years right after 1735 the platform fervor of Edwards, Whitefield and Wesley changed a generation. After the spiritual coldness of the American Revolution, the Second Great Awakening changed both seaboard and frontier, although fiery preaching seems more a result than a cause of the revival. Whatever his theology, Finney's preaching left its mark in conversions and changed lives. The revivals of 1858, 1875, 1910, and the years after the Great War were marked by great preaching. If we rest on the sovereign will of God, we at least know that He has the power. As the leper said to the Lord, "Lord,

A Last Word

if thou wilt, thou canst" (Matt. 8:2).

We have to believe in the power of God to grip our own hearts. If we are going to preach earnestly, it will not be as we are swept along by religious movements outside ourselves. Our passion will come from within, as the Spirit of God working in us generates an ever-fresh love for the Lord, a gratitude for the forgiveness of sins, an awareness of the awful destiny of the lost and a wonder at the greatness of God and the sweetness of His fellowship.

It remains to us to approach the Throne in believing prayer. With the temple veil rent in two, we have the privilege of access every waking moment we live. We appropriate by personal experience the forgiveness that the altar expresses and the cleansing that the laver pictures. We come to Christ as our Living Bread (John 6:35), and we acknowledge Him as our Light. At the altar of incense we accept Him as our Intercessor. When we have spiritually done all those, we remember that on that basis we have the sweet joy of communion with God, as pictured by the ark and the mercy seat.

As the prophets were known as men of God, so should the preachers of every generation appear. Homiletics is more than methods and techniques, nuts and bolts. Homiletics, rightly viewed, is the total of all that a preacher does as he prepares and conveys God's message to men. Homiletics includes clear exegesis and exposition, logical organization, good argument and illustration. In addition to all that, however, homiletics includes the experience in prayer by which the preacher qualifies, not as a performer but as a man of God.

When the Council told Peter and John to quit preaching, they answered, "Whether it be right in the sight of God to hearken unto you more than unto God, judge ye. For we cannot but speak the things which we have seen and heard" (Acts 4:19, 20).

May it be the same with us.